LAW
OF
ADOPTION

by MORTON L. LEAVY &
ROY D. WEINBERG

*This Legal Almanac has been revised
by the Oceana Editorial Board*

Irving J. Sloan
General Editor

FOURTH EDITION

1979
OCEANA PUBLICATIONS, INC.
Dobbs Ferry, New York

Library of Congress Cataloging in Publication Data

Leavy, Morton L.
    Law of adoption.

    (Legal almanac series ; no. 3)
    Includes index.
    1. Adoption— United States.   I. Weinberg,
Roy David, joint author.   II. Title.
KF545.Z95L4   1979   344'.73'032734   79-1157
ISBN: 0-379-11127-6

CONTENTS

INTRODUCTION

Properly speaking a legal adoption is a procedure which establishes the relationship of parent and child between persons not so related by nature. At the same time the adoption terminates all such relationships between the child and its natural parents.

Ordinarily adoption is a judicial proceeding, requiring a hearing before a judge of a competent court in the particular jurisdiction. In some states, however, an exception is made in the case of a father wishing to "adopt" an illegitimate child. In these jurisdictions a father may adopt an illegitimate child merely by publicly acknowledging that the child is his own, without being required to go through extended judicial proceedings.

Although ordinarily thought of as a relatively modern practice, adoption in fact has a history of great antiquity. Although unknown to the common law, the practice prevailed among the ancient Greeks, Romans, Babylonians and Assyrians.

The first American jurisdiction to enact an adoption statute was Massachusetts—in 1851. Prior to this, as well as later in many jurisdictions, adoptions, were negotiated by deed—a now obsolete practice. The first English adoption statute was enacted in 1926.

Originally, the primary purpose of adoption was to provide the adopting parent or parents with an heir, but today it embraces many other aspects of the parent-child relationship. In this connection it may be noted that the term "adoption" is often employed loosely and inaccurately, as, for example, in references to the sponsoring of alien refugees and orphans, when what is actually meant is merely that the sponsor is assuring or contributing to the alien's support after arrival in this country.

Modern adoption procedures are primarily designed for protection of the interests and welfare of the adoptee, but they simultaneously safeguard those of the adopting and natural parents.

As in the case of marriage, divorce and other aspects of family law, adoption practice is governed by state or territorial law rather than federal. Each state has its own adoption statute and while many of such laws correspond in essentials, no two are identical. Even Montana and Oklahoma, the two states which have adopted the Uniform Act, have incorporated varying modifications.

The law of the forum state governs adoption proceedings even when some of the parties reside elsewhere. In many states the procedure is explained in pamphlets provided by the state welfare department. Where adoptions are handled through child placement agencies, advice respecting the proper procedure may be obtained through such organizations.

It should be remembered that adoption procedure, as specified in the pertinent state statute, must be strictly followed and that a legally binding adoption must be one in which all the formal requirements have been satisfied.

As adoption almost always involves the preparation of legal documents, as well as a formal hearing in court, the advice and service of a competent attorney is usually essential. In some instances legal assistance may be obtained from public officials. In Arizona, for example, it is provided that the county attorney shall give legal assistance without charge to persons desiring to institute adoption proceedings. For the most part, however, the services of a private practitioner will be necessary.

It is ordinarily desirable to seek the guidance of an attorney or authorized agency as soon as a decision to adopt is made, even though there has been as yet no choice of a child. Such persons will be able to tell the prospective petitioner whether he can qualify as an adopter pursuant to the pertinent law, the nature of the proceedings in general and the ultimate effect of adoption. It should be remembered, however, that the fuctions of an attorney and a placement agency are entirely distinct and that neither should undertake to assume those of the other.

These and related matters are considered throughout the course of this volume, whose primary purpose is to give prospective adopters a general understanding of the pertinent law. It is not intended, nor should it be used, as a substitute for competent legal or adoption agency advice. In fact, the utilization of expert counsel and assistance at the earliest possible moment frequently saves adopting parents both time and money and enables them to avoid much misery and heartache.

Chapter 1

HISTORY OF ADOPTION

Among the ancient peoples of Greece, Rome, Egypt and Babylonia, adoption served essentially as a way of providing a male heir to childless couples. Male children were considered crucial not only to maintain the family line for inheritance of property, but also for performance of religious rites. In Rome, an additional function of adoption was related to the notion that a candidate for public office was better if he had children, or had more of them, than his opponent. In these ancient cultures, the adopted were often adult citizens instead of abandoned or destitute children. A man might adopt his daughter's husband or her sons to carry on the family line. In early Rome it was customary for a large family to allow one of its sons to be adopted by a childless family, thereby forming a closer alliance between the two families and providing an heir to the second family.

Inheritance

Inheritance is still of such importance that in countries such as France, Greece, Spain and most of Latin America, adoption is prohibited when it would change the inheritance rights of biological children.

The pactice of adoption disappeared almost completely in Europe in the Middle Ages. The most common means of transferring custody of a child was through indenture. Indenturing treated the child as property, contracting him out to a work home until the age of majority (18 for girls, 21 for boys), usually in exchange for food, clothing, and housing, as well as basic schooling and some training in an occupation. Until adoption was introduced again with the general adoption laws passed in the mid-nineteenth century, the few adoptions that did take place were either informal agreements or by means of a separate legislative act for each particular child being adopted by each particular adult.

Formal legal provisions of a general adoption law was an outgrowth of concern such as that voiced in a report by the New York Commissioners of the Code in 1865 recommending enactment of general adoption law in New York State. While informal adoptions were not uncommon, adopting parents feared that

1

natural parents would reclaim children, especially if there was a financial advantage. The Report stated:

> ". . . yet there is no method by which the adopting parents can secure the children to themselves except by a fictitious apprenticeship, a form which, when applied to children in the cradle, becomes absurd and repulsive. It is, indeed, so inappropriate a form in every case that it is rarely resorted to."

The first general adoption statutes in the United States were passed in 1850 in Texas and Vermont. These and laws enacted shortly after by a few other states were passed merely to "make public record of private agreements of adoptions." There was no mention of public supervision or requirement that a judgment be made on the propriety of the adoption.

In 1851 Massachusetts was the first of several states, including New York, to enact a law which provided to some extent for judicial supervision, calling for a judgment to be made of the parents' ability to provide for the child.

From 1890 through the 1920's many states passed laws that provided for social investigations to be either prerequisites in all adoptions or required at the discretion of the judges. In many cases these social investigations were delegated to county departments of charity or welfare.

The practice of adoption in this country has evolved from the needs of childless parents to a focus on the needs of parentless children. In addition to the social investigation of prospective adoptive homes, waiting periods have been imposed between the child's placement in a home and the legal consumation of the adoption. In many states, once the adoption proceedings are closed, records are sealed and a new birth certificate is issued in order to protect the rights of the child and his adoptive parents.

Chapter 2

QUALIFICATIONS OF ADOPTING PERSONS

As a general rule, adoption may be undertaken by either married or unmarried persons, and the requirements are basically the same in either case. In the case of the former, however, all states require either that the petition be made jointly or be consented to by the other spouse. The requirement of a joint petition, however, does not apply in connection with the adoption of a stepchild: the petition is submitted solely by the stepparent, with the consent of the spouse (the natural parent).

AGE: The most commonly encountered age requirement is that the adopting parent be at least 21 years of age. Many statutes merely specify "any adult" or "any person of lawful age", but the usual effect of this provision is as just stated. There are, however, jurisdictional variants to this general rule. Some states setting a minimum age of 21 nevertheless permit married persons under that age to join in an adoption petition, while a number of states allow "any person" or "any resident" to adopt (making it possible for minors to institute adoption proceedings). In some jurisdictions, the adopting parent must be a specified number of years older than the adopted child. Eight states, for example, require that this age differential be at least 10 years. In two states, the differential is 15 years (unless the adoptee be the child of the adopter's spouse). In Georgia, an adopter must be 25 years of age if unmarried (otherwise, an "adult") and at least 10 years older than the child. Puerto Rico has a unique provision that the adopting parent be over 21 years of age and also 16 years older than the adopted child, except in a stepchild adoption where the adopter has been married to the adoptee's parent for at least five years.

3

Chart A (which follows) lists the statutory requirements in this connection. It specifies the persons who may adopt and the prescribed age limitations. It should be remembered, however, that in agency adoptions age requirements may be more stringent than those specified by statute. Many responsible agencies set a maximum age for adopting parents at about 40 years particularly where infants are involved. Such requirements may be ascertained by consulting the particular adoption agencies.

Chart A

WHO MAY ADOPT

STATE	Statutory Definition	Other Age Requirements
Alabama	Proper adult	-
Alaska	Any person	-
Arizona	Any adult	10 years older than child
Arkansas	Any person of lawful age	-
California	Any adult	10 years older than child
Colorado	Any person	Over 21
Connecticut	Any person	18 years of age
Delaware	Any resident	Over 21 if unmarried
District of Columbia	Any person	-
Florida	Any adult	-
Georgia	Adult resident (married and living with spouse; 25 years of age if unmarried)	10 years older than child

4

STATE	Statutory Definition	Other Age Requirements
Hawaii	Any proper adult person	-
Idaho	Any adult	15 years older than child (unless spouse of natural parent)
Illinois	Any reputable person	Of legal age, but minor may adopt by leave of court for good cause
Indiana	Any resident	-
Iowa	Any person of lawful age (construed to include minors attaining majority by marriage)	-
Kansas	Any adult	-
Kentucky	Any adult resident	-
Louisiana	Any person	Over 21 if unmarried; person over 20 may adopt person over 17
Maine	Any person	-
Maryland	Any person	Over 21
Massachusetts	Person of full age	Other than adoptee
Michigan	Any person	-
Minnesota	Any resident of more than one year (unless requirement waived)	-
Mississippi	Any proper unmarried adult, or spouses jointly	-
Missouri	Any person	-

STATE	Statutory Definition	Other Age Requirements
Montana	Spouses jointly; either if other is child's parent; single person 21 years of age; unmarried parent of illegitimate child; married person of 21 and legally separated	Adopter of adult must be 10 years older than adoptee
Nebraska	Any adult	-
Nevada	Any adult or any married couple	10 years older than child
New Hampshire	Any person may adopt minor; any adult may adopt adult unless latter is spouse, brother, sister, uncle or aunt of whole or half blood	-
New Jersey	Any adult U.S. citizen (or one who has declared intent to be)	10 years older than child (15, if adult adoptee)
New Mexico	Bona fide resident, or non-resident relative within third degree	20 years older if adopting adult
New York	Any adult (minor may adopt spouse's child born in or out of wedlock)	-
North Carolina	Any proper adult person or spouses jointly	-
North Dakota	Any adult	10 years older than adoptee
Ohio	Any proper person	

6

STATE	Statutory Definition	Other Age Requirements
Oklahoma	Spouses jointly; either if other is child's parent; single person 21 years of age; married parent of illegitimate child; married person of 21 and legally separated	-
Oregon	Any person	-
Pennsylvania	Any adult	-
Puerto Rico	Any person in full exercise of civil rights	Over 21 and 16 years older than adoptee (except in stepchild adoption by spouse of at least 5 years)
Rhode Island	Any person	Older than adoptee
South Carolina	Spouses jointly; either if other is parent of child; single person of legal age; married, of legal age and legally separated; any unmarried parent may adopt illegitimate child	Only adult may adopt adult
South Dakota	Any adult	10 years older than child
Tennessee	Any U.S. citizen	Over 21
Texas	Any adult	-
Utah	Any adult	10 years older than child
Vermont	Any person of age and sound mind	
Virginia	Any natural person	

STATE	Statutory Definition	Other Age Requirements
Washington	Any person	-
West Virginia	Any person	15 years older than child (unless stepchild)
Wisconsin	Any adult resident; resident spouses (or resident stepparent) may adopt minor	-
Wyoming	Any resident (of 21) (or spouses jointly or either if stepparent) (any person may adopt adult resident)	-

RESIDENCE: In the ordinary case where both the child and adopting parents live in the same state, resident requirements present no problems. Various complications may arise, however, when this is not the case. There are two possible solutions:
1. The child may be brought into the state where the adopting parents reside.
2. The adopting parents may go to the state where the child resides and bring the adoption proceedings there.

In deciding upon which course to follow, attention must be given to both legal and practical considerations. If possible, it is generally preferable to institute the proceeding in the state where the adopting parents reside. The chief reason for this is that the court considering the application will be in a better position to obtain pertinent information and evidence concerning the prospective adopters and thus properly determine whether or not to approve the application. In addition, if, as is usually the case, an official investigation is required before an application may be approved, it greatly simplifies matters if the proceeding is in the state where the petitioners reside. However, it may be difficult or impossible for either legal or practical reasons to bring the proceeding in this jurisdiction. For example, if the child is in a boarding home or agency in another state, it will be necessary to secure the assitance and cooperation of those having custody of the child in order to transport the latter to the forum state for purposes of adoption. Moreover, consideration must be given to the various state laws respecting the interstate

8

transportation of children for purposes of adoption. Most states have such laws, and in practically all of these, it is necessary to first obtain permission from the state welfare department. Most also require the posting of a bond, usually for $1,000, although in some states it is higher. About half the states which regulate importation require, in addition to permission from the state welfare department, follow-up reports to that agency.

A few states regulate exportation, i.e., the taking of a child out of a state for adoption. These laws are generally simpler than those relating to importation. Permission from the state welfare agency is usually required, and sometimes follow-up reports, but generally no bond-filing requirement. Moreover, the exportation laws do not usually apply where the child is taken from the state by its parents or guardian.

In addition to the laws just described are others which may demand attention in certain situations. Where, as is occurring with increased frequency, children are brought to this country for adoption from abroad, consideration must be given to the laws of the country of origin as well as to our own immigration requirements.

If it cannot conveniently be arranged to bring the proceeding where the adopting parents reside, the only alternative is to proceed in the state where the child resides if this is legally feasible. However, some states require that adopters be residents thereof, while some go even further and require residence for a stated period of time prior to instituting an adoption proceeding.

The following chart (Chart B) lists the residence requirements (if any) of the various states.

9

Chart B

RESIDENCE REQUIREMENTS FOR
ADOPTING PARENTS

STATE	Are There Residence Requirements?	What Are They?
Alabama	No	-
Alaska	No	-
Arizona	Yes	Residence of State
Arkansas	No	-
California	Yes	Residence of County of Proceeding
Colorado	No	-
Connecticut	No	-
Delaware	Yes	Resident of State
District of Columbia	Yes	Legal Resident of District or Have Lived One Year in District (unless adoptee in legal custody or control of Commissioners or child-placement agency)
Florida	Yes	Resident of State
Georgia	Yes	Resident of State
Hawaii	No	-
Idaho	Yes	Resident of and residing in State
Illinois	Yes	6 Months Immediate Continuous Residence (no residence requirement if adoptee is "related child" or child placed by an "agency")

STATE	Are There Residence Requirements?	What Are They?
Indiana	Yes	Residence of State
Iowa	No	-
Kansas	No	-
Kentucky	Yes	Resident of State or lived 12 months next preceding in State
Louisiana	No	-
Maine	No	-
Maryland	No	-
Massachusetts	No	-
Michigan	Yes	Resident of State
Minnesota	Yes	Resident of State for at least One Year (waivable by Court for best interests of child)
Mississippi	Yes	Resident of State for 90 Days before filing Petition (unless child related to one of the petitioners within third degree under civil law)
Missouri	No	-
Montana	Yes	Resident of State
Nebraska	Yes	Resident of State
Nevada	Yes	Reside in State for Six months before Granting of Adoption
New Hampshire	No (but non-resident can't adopt illegitimate child whose mother was non-resident at child's birth, unless she resided in state (N.H.) at least six months when petition filed)	

11

STATE	Are There Residence Requirements?	What Are They?
New Jersey	No	-
New Mexico	Yes (Generally)	Bona-fide Resident of State (except for relatives within third degree)
New York	No	-
North Carolina	Yes	Resided in State or Federal Territory therein One Year just before filing Petition (residence, but not one year requirement applies in step-child adoption)
North Dakota	Yes (Generally)	Resident of State (unless relative)
Ohio	No	-
Oklahoma	Yes	Resident of State
Oregon	No	-
Pennsylvania	No	-
Puerto Rico	Yes	Resided in Puerto Rico Six months before Date of Petition
Rhode Island	Yes	Resident of State
South Carolina	No	-
South Dakota	No	-
Tennessee	Yes	Lived or maintained regular Place of Abode in State for One Year, regardless of Legal Residence (if in military service—one year before entering service)
Texas	No (child adoption)	Adult Adoption of Adult (Resident of State

STATE	Are There Residence Requirements?	What Are They?
Utah	Yes	Resident of State
Vermont	No	-
Virginia	Yes	Resident of State (or has custody of child placed by Virginia child-placement agency)
Washington	No	-
West Virginia	Yes	Resident of State
Wisconsin	Yes	Resident of State
Wyoming	Yes	Resident of State (but any person may adopt adult resident)

This brief discussion of residence requirements emphasizes the many serious questions to be considered when a child and its would-be adopters reside in different jurisdictions. It should be noted, however, that, wherever an adoption proceeding is brought, the decree will ordinarily be recognized in all sister states—provided, of course, that all legal requirements of the issuing state have been met. This is in accordance with the "full faith and credit" provisions of the Federal Constitution. Some states have statutes specifically providing for the legality and recognition of out-of-state adoptions.

Chapter 3

PERSONS WHO MAY BE ADOPTED

Minor Children

All state laws provide for the adoption of minors. This is generally true whether or not the child's natural parents are alive. As noted later, however, the consent of living natural parents is usually required. A minor is ordinarily defined as a child under 21 years of age, although a different age limitation obtains in a few states.

Adults

The vast majority of adoptions, of course, are of children. Adult adoption, however, is permissible in most, but not all of the states. It is ordinarily much simpler to adopt an adult than a minor. Adoption statutes in general are designed to protect the interests of the child and insure, insofar as possible, that it will be placed in a suitable home. An adult, of course, does not require the same degree of protection. Hence, many of the more stringent provisions are often eliminated in adult adoption proceedings, and in some states, the simplified procedures also apply to married minors.

Chart C, which follows, indicates, in broad outline, the varying state statutes with respect to who may be adopted.

Chart C

WHO MAY BE ADOPTED

STATE	Minors?	Adults?	Persons of Any Age?
Alabama	X		
Alaska	X	X	
Arizona	X		
Arkansas			X
California	X	X (younger than adopter; can't adopt spouse)	
Colorado	X	X	
Connecticut	X	X (younger than adopter) (must have consent of adoptee's adult spouse)	
Delaware	X	X	
District of Columbia	X	X	
Florida	X	X (over 10 years younger than adopter)	
Georgia	X	X	
Hawaii	X		

Chart C (Continued)

STATE	Minors?	Adults?	Persons of Any Age?
Idaho	X	X (where adoption not made during minority due to inadvertence, mistake or neglect and adopter has had relation of parent for over 15 years continuously)	
Illinois	X	X (if lived in home of adopter at any time for two years continuously before adoption proceeding, or related in manner of a "related child")	
Indiana	X	X	
Iowa	X	X	
Kansas	X	X	
Kentucky			X
Louisiana	X	X	
Maine			X
Maryland	X	X	

Chart C (Continued)

STATE	Minors?	Adults?	Persons of Any Age?
Massachusetts			X (younger than adopter)
Michigan	X		
Minnesota	X	X	
Mississippi	X	X	
Missouri			X
Montana	X (any child present in state when petition filed)	X (10 years younger than adopter)	
Nebraska	X		
Nevada	X	X (younger than adopter)	
New Hampshire	X	X	
New Jersey	X	X	
New Mexico	X (living in state when petition filed)	X (unmarried, childless, and 20 years younger than adopter)	
New York			X
North Carolina	X		
North Dakota	X	X	

17

Chart C (Continued)

STATE	Minors?	Adults?	Persons of Any Age?
Ohio	X		
Oklahoma	X (any child present in state when petition filed)	X	
Oregon			X
Pennsylvania	X	X	
Puerto Rico			X
Rhode Island			X (younger than adopter)
South Carolina	X	X (by adult)	
South Dakota	X	X (by adult with written consent of adoptee who has lived in a-dopter's home for six months during minority)	
Tennessee			X (for children over 18, only adoptee's consent required unless adjudicated non-com-

18

Chart C (Continued)

STATE	Minors?	Adults?	Persons of Any Age?
Tennessee (cont'd.)			pos mentis (guardian's consent required)
Texas	X	X	
Utah	X	X (whose parents are both dead)	
Vermont			X
Virginia	X	X (stepchild of at least one year; niece or nephew with no living parents who has lived in adopter's home for at least one year; any adult who has resided in adopter's home for at least five years before reaching majority)	
Washington			X
West Virginia	X	X	
Wisconsin			X
Wyoming	X	X (resident)	

RACIAL AND RELIGIOUS LIMITATIONS: A frequently encountered obstacle to adoption is met when the parties are of different races or religions. In this connection, it may be observed that serious constitutional questions may be involved, particularly in light of a recent Supreme Court invalidation of a statute outlawing interracial marriage. In the case of adoption, however, such questions have not as yet been subjected to definitive judicial determination.

Agencies which place children for adoption frequently will not approve interracial or interreligious adoptions. Some statutes specifically prohibit "mixed" adoption proceedings. In Louisiana, for example, the law requires that the child and adopting parents be of the same race. Texas specifically prohibits Negro-White adoptions. In some states, the petition or investigative committee report, or both, must state the race or color and/or religion of the child and adopting parents. Even where the statutes are silent on the subject, the court may refuse to approve a "mixed" adoption (racial or religious) on the theory that such an adoption is not in the best interests of the child. This applies particularly to interracial adoptions which are rarely, if ever, approved by Southern courts.

Many states require by law that the child be adopted into a family of the same religious faith, and as a practical matter, this policy is followed almost uniformly by child-placement agencies. Numerous state statutes deal specifically with the matter of the religion of the parties, but these vary considerably in detail. Some require that "due consideration" be given to the matter; others that the religions be the same "whereever possible"; and still others provide additional tests to be applied. Many provide that the petitioner incorporate information as to race and religion in his petition. In addition to legislative policy and judicial precedent, the manuals of many state welfare departments as well as private agencies indicate that considerable attention will be given to both race and religion when an adoption placement is made.

Statutes bearing on the question of religious and racial characteristics of adopter and adoptee are many and varied. It is instructive to examine a few of these. In Delaware, for example, one of the adoptive parents must be of the same religion as the prospective adoptee's natural mother unless the latter, in a notarized statement, specifies the religion in which she desires the child to be brought up or states that she has no religion. Florida law specifies that "when practicable" the child and the adopters should be of the same religion, but the mother may give her written consent to placement with adopters of a different religion. Illinois also requires identity to religion "whenever practicable," but this requirement applies only to agency placements, not private. As already noted, in Louisiana, adoptees must be of the same race as their adopters. The Maryland law is similar to that of Florida with respect to this question. Massachusetts requires identity of religion "when practicable" regardless of the mother's intent. Technically the court has a right to grant a mixed adoption, but is supposed to do so only upon the placement agency's recommendation. As the agency's own rules ordinarily prohibit mixed adoptions, such an adoption is possible only when the court disregards the agency's recommendation. When it does so, it must state in writing the reasons therefor. and these become part of the minutes of the proceedings.

In Missouri if the child bears any signs of coming from a different race than that of the adopters within a period of five years, the adoption may be set aside. In Ohio, the investigating agency "takes into account" the racial, religious and cultural background of the child and the adopters. New York law is similar to that of Massachusetts in regard to religion. Pennsylvania provides that "whenever possible" the child should be of the same religion as the adopter; otherwise, the court requires the mother to appear and state her approval to the mixed adoption. The Rhode Island statute is similar to those of Massachusetts and New York, but somewhat stricter. The court is forbidden to grant a mixed adoption if anyone else of the child's religion can be found in the state who will adopt it. Where a mixed adoption is granted, the court must state the reasons and these then become a part of the minutes of the proceeding. It has been noted that in Texas a white person may not adopt a Negro, nor may a Negro adopt a white person.

Placement Statutes

As noted in an earlier connection, all adoption statutes at present provide for some sort of investigation, either mandatory or discretionary. In the case of private placements, the investigation commonly comes after the child has lived in the home of the wouldbe adopters for a substantial period of time. This frequently results in judicial approval of otherwise unsatisfactory adoptions, since the courts are reluctant to sever family ties already formed. In order to remedy this defect in the law, many states have enacted placement

21

statutes which either prohibit independent placements altogether or subject them to specific requirements.

The following states have outlawed nonrelative adoptions: Alabama, California, Connecticut, Delaware, Montana, New York, North Dakota, Oregon, South Dakota, Texas, Virginia and Wisconsin (also the District of Columbia). The Ohio statute provides that no child "shall be placed or received for adoption or with intent to adopt except through a placement made by a county welfare department having a child welfare division . . . or an organization authorized to place children . . . unless prior to such placement . . . the parent or parents . . . have personally applied to, and appeared before, the probate court of the county in which such child is then a resident for approval of the proposed placement . . . and unless said court, after an independent investigation . . . has determined that it is in the best interests of the child and has approved of record the proposed placement."

Other states have even stricter statutes prohibiting private placements with anyone other than a relative, e.g., Colorado, Georgia, Indiana, Maine and Tennessee. Still other jurisdictions require notification to the state welfare department in the case of private placements. Maryland and New Hampshire require notification by the prospective adopters. Rhode Island and Kentucky in effect require notification by the party making the placement, while Massachusetts places this burden on both. It should be noted, however, that many of these laws are flouted with impunity because of the reluctance to prosecute in the face of already overworked agencies.

Chapter 4

JURISDICTION OF THE COURT

A matter of prime importance in connection with an adoption proceeding is familiarity with the court in which it should be brought. Where, as noted earlier, the parties reside in different jurisdictions, the first decision will be the choice of state in which to proceed. Oftentimes, however, there is no choice because of the particular state requirements. There are really two questions involved in identification of the proper court:

1. The court invested with competent jurisdiction, and its name.
2. The proper venue, i.e., the county (or, occasionally, city) in which the proceeding may be instituted.

CLASS OF COURT: Under the judicial systems established in this country, each court generally can entertain only certain types of cases. For example, some courts may hear only criminal cases; some, only civil cases; still others, only matters of probate and decedents' estates. It is imperative, therefore, to first determine which class of court in each state may   entertain and dispose of adoption proceedings.

Ordinarily, there is but one type of court in each state which may hear and adjudicate adoption proceedings. Usually such proceedings are brought in courts having jurisdiction over wills and decedents' estate or those with specific jurisdiction over family or children's proceedings. These tribunals have varying names in different jurisdictions. In some states, adoption cases are heard by Probate courts; in others, by the District Court; in still others, the Juvenile Court, Superior Court, or Surrogate's Court.

In a handful of states, more than one class of court may entertain adoption proceedings.

VENUE: After ascertaining the appropriate court in which to proceed, it is still necessary to determine the proper venue, i.e., in which county to bring the action. This problem arises, for example, when the adopting parents reside in one part of the state and the child in another. In about half of the states, there is no choice, the statutes specifying the venue—generally the county where the petitioning, adopting parents reside. The basic reason for this is that it is usually easier to conduct an investigation into their fitness to provide a suitable home. In the remaining states, the adopting parents have a choice of venue, ordinarily limited to either the county where the adopters reside or the child resides. In some jurisdictions, it is also provided that when the child is in the custody of a child-caring agency or similar organization, the proceeding may be brought in the county where such agency is located. Even where such choices are available, however, it is usually preferable to bring the proceedings in the county where the petitioner resides.

Chart D gives the name of the court in each state where adoption proceedings may be brought, also indicating the availability of a choice, and, where present, its nature.

The letter "P" appearing in columns headed "Where" denotes that the proceeding may be brought in the place indicated (e.g., "Where Agency having Child Is Located"). Exceptional provisions are listed in the footnotes.

Chart D

PROPER COURT IN ADOPTION PROCEEDINGS

STATE	Court	Does Petitioner Have a Choice of Venue?	Where Petitioner Resides?	Where Child Resides?	Where Agency having Child Located?
Alabama	Probate	Yes	P	P(1)	P
Alaska	Superior	Yes	P (statewide venue)	P	
Arizona	Superior	No	P		
Arkansas	Probate	No		P(2)	
California	Superior	No	P		
Colorado	Juvenile, if functioning; otherwise County(3)	Yes	P	P	P
Connecticut	Probate	No	P(4)		
Delaware	Orphans'	No	P		
District of Columbia	Domestic Relations Branch of Court of General Sessions	No			

Chart D (Continued)

STATE	Court	Does Petitioner Have a Choice of Venue?	Where Petitioner Resides?	Where Child Resides?	Where Agency having Child Located?
Florida	Circuit	Yes	P	P	P
Georgia	Superior	No (generally)	P(5)		
Hawaii	Circuit	Yes	P	P	
Idaho	Probate	No	P		
Illinois	Circuit	Yes	P	P (or was born; or where parents reside; or any county if in custody of agency or has guardian)	
Indiana	County Ct. with Probate Jurisdiction	Yes	P	P	
Iowa	District	Yes	P	P	
Kansas	Probate	No	P(6)	P(6)	
Kentucky	Circuit	No	P		

Louisiana	Juvenile or District	Yes	P(7)	
Maine	Probate	No	P(8)	P(8)
Maryland	Circuit Ct. sitting in Equity (9)	Yes	P	P
Massachusetts	Probate	No	P(8)	P(8)
Michigan	Probate	No	P	
Minnesota	Juvenile	No	P	
Mississippi	Chancery	Yes	P	P (or where born or found when deserted or abandoned; or where home to which child surrendered located)
Missouri	Circuit (juvenile division)	Yes	P	P
Montana	District	No	P	
Nebraska	County	No	P	
Nevada	District	Yes (child: any county; adult adoption: county of either adopter's or adoptee's residence)		

Chart D (Continued)

STATE	Court	Does Petitioner Have a Choice of Venue?	Where Petitioner Resides?	Where Child Resides?	Where Agency having Child Located?
New Hampshire	Probate	Yes	P	P	
New Jersey	Superior, Juvenile and Domestic Relations, or County Ct. if parents were divorced in state, unless said court has awarded custody to agency or consented to proceeding in other said courts)	Yes	P	P	P (if adult adoptee) (where agency has principal office)
New Mexico	District (child a-doption) District and Probate (adult adoption)	No	P	P	
New York	Family	No	P(6)	P(6)	P(6)
North Carolina	Superior	Yes	P	P(1)	P
North Dakota	District	No	P(8)	P(8)	
Ohio	Probate	Yes	P(11)	P(11)	
Oklahoma	County (or Children's Ct., if existant)	No	P		

State	Court				
Oregon	County (or other court of competent jurisdiction)	No	P(7)	P	P
Pennsylvania Philadelphia—Philadelphia)	Orphans' Ct. (in Municipal Ct. of Philadelphia)	Yes	P	P(12)	P
Puerto Rico	Superior	No		no restrictions	
Rhode Island under 18); Probate (adoptee over 18)	Juvenile (adoptee	No / Yes (where adoptee over 18)	P (adoptee under 18)	P	P
South Carolina court with concurrent jurisdiction	Common Pleas or	Yes	P	P (whether petitioner resident or non-resident)	P (if petitioner non-resident)
South Dakota	County	Yes	P	P	P
Tennessee	Chancery (or Circuit)	Yes(13)	P	P(1)	P
Texas	District	Yes	P	P	P
Utah	District	No	P	P	
Vermont	Probate	No	P(6)	P(6)	P(6)

Chart D (Continued)

STATE	Court	Does Petitioner Have a Choice of Venue?	Where Petitioner Resides?	Where Child Resides?	Where Agency having Child Located?
Virginia	Court of record with Chancery jurisdiction	No(14)	P		P
Washington	Superior	Yes	P	P	
West Virginia	Circuit (Juvenile court where Circuit Ct. does not sit as Juvenile Ct.)	No	P		
Wisconsin	County	No	P (adoption of adults)	P (adoption of minors)	
Wyoming	District	No	P		

FOOTNOTES TO CHART D

(1) In the states so marked, it is provided that if the child is a public charge, the adoption proceeding may be brought at the place where the child resided when it became a public charge.

(2) In Arkansas, the proceeding may be brought in the county court in cases of destitute, delinquent, homeless or abandoned children.

(3) In Colorado, the proper court for the adoption of adults is the county or district court of either the adopter's or adoptee's residence.

(4) In Connecticut, if the child is in an institution, the petition is filed in the district where the institution is located. If not in an institution, the child may be adopted by proceedings in the district where the petitioner resides.

(5) In Georgia, the court may, for good cause, permit the petition to be filed in the county where the child placing agency is located or where the child is domiciled.

(6) In Kansas, New York and Vermont, the proceeding is brought in the county of residence of the petitioner; if he be a nonresident of the state, then in the county where the child resides, or if the child is in or being adopted from an institution, then in the county where it is located.

(7) Or where parents (or legal custodian) reside.

(8) In these states, the proceeding is brought in the county where the petitioner lives, if a resident of the state, or in the county where the child lives, if the petitioner is a nonresident.

(9) In Baltimore City, the proceedings are brought in Equity Court.

(10) If the petitioner is a nonresident.

(11) In Ohio, the proceeding may also be brought in the county where the child was born, has a legal settlement, or has become a public charge.

(12) With the court's permission.

(13) But the State Attorney General has ruled that the petition should ordinarily be brought where the petitioner lives.

(14) If the petitioner resides in the City of Richmond, and north of James River, the petition is brought in the Chancery Court of the City of Richmond; if petitioner resides south of James River, then in Hustings Court of the City of Richmond, Part II.

Editor's Note: *The petition in the case of an agency placement adoption is essentially the same except for allegations appropriate to that type of adoption (with respect to such matters as consent, etc.).*

Chapter 5

INITIATING ADOPTION PROCEDURES

Adoption proceedings are begun by filing in the proper court a formal document known as a petition. In some states a written agreement of adoption must be filed with the petition. The petition is signed by the persons seeking to adopt and sets forth appropriate information respecting the child, its natural parents, and the adopting parents, and requests the court to approve the adoption. It may also include a request for a change of the child's name, if this should be desired.

The state statutes usually indicate specifically what information should be included in the petition. While these statutes vary in detail, the information generally required is as follows:

As to the Child:

1. Name, residence, and age or date of birth.
2. A description of property, if any, possessed by the child.
3. If the child is in the custody of an agency or organization, a statement as to how such custody was acquired.
4. If a guardian has been appointed in place of the natural parents, his name and address is usually required.
5. In addition, many states require information as to sex, race, religion, place of birth, length of time the child has resided with the adopting parents, how the child came to their home, etc.

As to the Natural Parents:

1. Name and residence, and perhaps additional information as to race, religion, marital status, etc. In many states, however, the name and address of the father need not be stated if the child is illegitimate.

As to the Adopting Parents:

1. Name, age, residence and marital status.
2. In many states, information as to race, religion, financial re-

sources, employment and other sources of income. In some states, certain consents (see Chapter 6) must be filed with the petition. In addition, documents concerning guardianship, relinquishment of rights of natural parents, commitment of child to agency or institution, and similar matters, may also have to be presented with the petition.

It should be noted that the adopting parents need not be citizens of the United States, except in Tennessee and New Jersey (where they must either be citizens or must have officially declared their intention of becoming such).

Being a legal document, the petition should be prepared by the attorney handling the proceeding for the prospective adopters. He will be conversant with the proper procedure and be able to advise with respect to information required to be included under the particular state law.

The documents which follow are examples of the type of petition commonly used in New York State. It is presented in order to give the reader some idea of the nature of a petition. It must be remembered, however, that the particular form used varies considerably from state to state.

FORM OF PETITION
TO ADOPT [1]

In the Matter of the Adoption of

. . . .   Docket No. . . . .

        (minor) (under)

A (person) (over)   the Age of

Fourteen years

Petition—Private

Placement [2]

TO the FAMILY COURT:

The undersigned petitioners respectfully show that:

1. Petitioners . . . . and . . . . the proposed foster parents are husband and wife and reside at . . . .(Petitioner . . . ., the (minor) (person) above named is over the age of eighteen years and resides with the aforesaid Petitioners at the place of residence aforestated).

2. The proposed foster parents are of full age, the said . . . . having been born on . . . . and the said . . . . having been born on . . . . were married to each other on . . . . .on . . . . at . . . . and are living together as husband and wife. (Petitioner . . . . was born on . . . . and is unmarried).

3. The proposed foster parents desire to adopt . . . . a (minor) (person) (under) (over) fourteen years of age who was born on . . . . at . . . .

([3])4. Petitioner . . . . is the natural . . . . of . . . . the proposed foster child.

(1) Reprinted by permission of the copyright owners from Bender's Forms for Civil Practice, published by Matthew Bender & Co., Inc., 235 East 45th Street, New York, New York 10017

(2) Official Form No. 6-2-4.

(3) Strike out if inapplicable.

34

5. The parents of said proposed foster child are . . . . the natural father, who (died on . . . .) (is living and resides at . . . .) and . . . . the natural mother, who (died on . . . . at . . . .) (is living and resides at . . . .).

6. The religious faith of the proposed foster parents is . . . . , and that of the proposed foster child is . . . . As nearly as the same can be ascertained, the religious faith of the natural father of the proposed foster child is . . . . and that of the natural mother of the said child is . . . .

7. The consents required by law have been obtained and will be submitted with this petition. The consent of . . . . is not required because:

. . . .

. . . .

8. The proposed foster child has resided with the proposed foster parents continuously since . . . . The manner in which said proposed foster parents obtained said proposed foster child is:

9. The occupation of the proposed foster father is . . . . and he has an approximate annual income of $ . . . . The occupation of the proposed foster mother is . . . . her business address is . . . . , and she has an approximate annual income of $ . . . .

10. Petitioners desire that the name by which the proposed foster child is to be known is . . . .

11. To the best of Petitioners' information and belief, there are no persons other than those hereinbefore mentioned interested in this proceeding (except . . . .

. . . .)

12. No previous application has been made to any court or judge for the relief sought herein (except . . . .

. . . .).

13. The said foster child has not previously been adopted. (Said foster child was previously adopted on the . . . . day of . . . . by an order of . . . . Court of . . . . duly entered in the

35

office of the .... on ...., a certified copy of which is annexed hereto and made part hereof).

WHEREFORE, your petitioners pray for an order allowing and confirming said adoption and allowing and stating that the said .... shall thenceforth be regarded and treated in all respects as the lawful child of the said .... and .... and be known by the name of .... together with such other and further relief as may be just and proper.

Dated: ....

....

VERIFICATION [1]

STATE OF NEW YORK)   ss:
County of . . . . ,)

. . . . and . . . . , being duly sworn depose and say: that they are the petitioners herein; that they have read the foregoing petition and know the contents thereof; that the same is true as to their own knowledge except as to matters therein stated to be alleged on information and belief and that as to those matters they believe it to be true.

. . . .
. . . .

Sworn to before me
  this . . . . day of . . . . 19 . . .
. . . .
(Deputy) Clerk of the Court
          Notary Public

Editor's Note: The petition in the case of an agency placement adoption is essentially the same except for allegations appropriate to that type of adoption (with respect to such matters as consent, etc.).

(1) Reprinted by permission of the copyright owners from *Bender's Forms for Civil Practice,* published by Matthew Bender & Co., Inc., 235 East 45th Street, New York, New York 10017

Chapter 6

CONSENTS AS PREREQUISITE

The consent of certain parties must be obtained before an adoption may be approved. While, here again, the various state laws differ in detail, the general classes of persons whose consents are required are much the same in all states. These fall into three separate groups:

1. The child—if deemed old enough to give consent.
2. The natural parents (or mother, if the child be illegitimate)—unless for good reasons, this consent may be dispensed with.
3. If the natural parents are dead, or their consents are unnecessary, the consent of the guardian, next of kin, "next friend" appointed by the court, or authorized agency to which the child has been surrendered.

In some states, the required consents are submitted together with the petition; in others, they may be given at the hearing.

CONSENT OF CHILD: In practically all states, consent of the child is required if he is legally old enough to consent. The only states in which this requirement does not obtain are Louisiana, New Jersey, and South Carolina. In a few states consent of the child may be waived.

The age at which a child is deemed sufficiently mature to consent varies among the several jurisdictions. In the majority of states, a child's consent is required if he is 14 years of age or more. In about one-third, the age is 12, while in three states and Puerto Rico, it is 10.

The following chart (Chart E) sets forth the varying age requirements relating to child consent and the states in which these obtain.

Chart E

CHILD'S CONSENT TO ADOPTION—
AGE REQUIREMENTS

10 Years

Maryland
Michigan
North Dakota (if between 10 and 14, court may waive written consent)
Puerto Rico (unless incapacitated)

12 Years

Arizona
California
Florida
Hawaii
Idaho
Kentucky (may be waived)
Massachusetts
Montana
New Mexico
North Carolina
Ohio (but not if child has resided continuously in adopting home for eight years or more, immediately before filing petition)
Oklahoma
Pennsylvania
South Dakota
Utah
West Virginia

No Requirements

Louisiana
New Jersey
South Carolina

14 Years

Alabama
Alaska
Arkansas
Connecticut
Delaware (may be waived by court
District of Columbia
Georgia
Illinois
Indiana
Iowa
Kansas (and of sound intellect)
Maine
Minnesota
Mississippi (or personal service of process on child)
Missouri (unless court finds insufficient mental capacity to consent)
Nebraska
Nevada
New Hampshire
New York (may be waived by court)
Oregon
Rhode Island
Tennessee
Texas
Vermont
Virginia
Washington
Wisconsin
Wyoming

CONSENT OF NATURAL PARENTS: While generally the consent of the living natural parents is required in adoption proceedings, it is important to note certain qualifications of this rule. At least half of the states have specific provisions covering cases where the child is illegitimate, usually eliminating, in such cases, the necessity of consent by the father. In a few states, the consent of the natural mother is sufficient unless the identity of the father is proved. Consent by the natural parents is almost uniformly dispensed with in cases where they have neglected, abandoned, or deserted the child; or have been deprived of custody judicially, or have voluntarily surrendered the child to a welfare agency; where they have been deprived of their civil rights or imprisoned for a felony; or are alcoholics. The same rule applies where the natural parents are unknown or missing. In other cases, where no such clearcut legal status exists, the court must determine the question from the attendant circumstances. In doubtful cases, the question of whether adoption is possible without the consent of the natural parents is one requiring the benefit of expert advice.

CONSENT OF GUARDIANS, AGENCIES, ETC.: If the natural parents are dead or their consent is unnecessary for reasons mentioned in the preceding discussion, the consent of a guardian or some other proper person will be required. If there be no guardian, the court will protect the interests of the child by requiring the consent of some substituted person or agency. Usually the State or some local Department of Public Welfare will be designated as the substitute. In some instances, the court will appoint a suitable person to act as the "friend" of the child. The pervading purpose is to insure that the adoption is in the best interests of the child and has been consented to by someone who has these interests at heart.

In many states provision is made whereby the natural parents may place the child in a licensed child-placement agency and sign a release of all rights. In such "surrenders" to child-placement agencies for adoption, subsequent consent by such natural parents to the adoption is unnecessary, but in order to fully protect the child's interest, the agency's consent is required. There is an increasing trend toward encouragement of such "surrenders" to agencies.

FORM OF CONSENT: There is considerable diversity among the jurisdictions as to the form of a consent. Some states require "consent", without denoting its exact nature; some require consent "in writing", and still others require that the consent be signed before the court (some specify any court of record). Most, however, merely require a consent acknowledged before a notary or officer empowered to take acknowledgments.

Chapter 7

JUDICIAL PROCEDURE AND HEARING

Notice

After the petition has been prepared and filed in court, notice of the adoption proceeding must be given. The question of notice is a highly technical one, and while the statutes of the various states differ considerably, as a general rule notice should be given to all persons whose consent is deemed necessary (see Chapter 6). There is a growing tendency to require that notice of the pending proceeding be given to the state or local Department of Welfare. Where personal service of notice cannot be made, provision is usually made for giving such notice by publication.

Investigation

Provisions for investigation prior to approval of adoption now exist in all jurisdictions. In most jurisdictions, these requirements are mandatory, although exemptions are recognized in some states where the parties occupy certain specified relationships.

Of course, where an adoption is arranged through a child-placement organization, it probably will have already conducted its own private investigation. In fact, in some states any person receiving a child for the purpose of making an adoption placement must file a preliminary report within 30 days. Where such a prior investigation has been made, the court, where permissible, will frequently appoint the same agency to conduct the official investigation.

The results of the official investigation are commonly included in a written report submitted to the court. Most state laws contain detailed provisions as to the information to be included in the report, although some merely provide that it should contain information about "the conditions and circumstances attending the adoption". Although here, too, there are considerable differences in detail among the various state laws and regulations, the general type of information appearing in such a report may be summarized as follows:

42

1. **About the Child**
   Its background, physical condition, mental condition, and other similar matters bearing upon its suitability for adoption.
2. **About the Adopting Parents**
   Their health, financial condition, fitness as parents; and suitability of their home for the child.
3. **About the Natural Parents**
   Why they desire to give up the child; whether they are unfit to be parents or have abandoned the child, etc.

Additional information as to race, religion, and national background of the parties is also required in many jurisdictions. In practice the reports submitted often go considerably beyond the minimum statutory requirements and include much additional data that the investigating agency regards as important.

In practically all states, the person or agency making the report is required to make a **recommendation** regarding the advisability of adoption in light of all the facts and circumstances of the particular case.

Chart F, which follows, contains a general summary of the requirements and parties responsible for investigation in the various jurisdictions.

Chart F
INVESTIGATION

STATE	Is Investigation Required?	Who Must Make?
Alabama	Yes	State Department of Public Welfare
Alaska	Yes (no specification, but inferrable from provision that no investigation required in adult adoptions)	
Arizona	Yes	Court officer or approved agency licensed by him
Arkansas	Yes (if ordered by Court)	Child Welfare Division
California	Yes (may be waived if adoption is through a licensed agency)	Department of Social Welfare
Colorado	Yes (except in relative or stepparent adoptions)	Any licensed placement age..; any public welfare dept.; or court's own probation dept.
Connecticut	Yes	Commissioner of Welfare
Delaware	Yes	State Board of Welfare or an authorized agency
District of Columbia	Yes	D.C. Board of Commissioners (licensed placement agency if supervising case)
Florida	Yes	Division of family services, department of health and rehabilitative services
Georgia	Yes	Dept. of Human Resources

State		
Hawaii	Yes (may be waived by Court)	Director of social services and housing (or nearest county administrator, or approved placement agency, if Director refers)
Idaho	Yes (in Court's discretion; unless petitioner related to child or married to natural par-	Department of health and welfare or qualified child-placement agency
Illinois	Yes	A licensed placement agency, a probation officer or (in Cook County) the County Services Division of the Cook County Department of Public Aid
Indiana	Yes	Duly licensed child-placement agency approved by State Dept. of Public Welfare
Iowa	Yes (may be waived by Court)	State Dept. of Social Welfare, or qualified person or agency named by Court
Kansas	Yes (discretionary in step-parent adoptions)	State Dept. of Social Welfare
Kentucky	Yes	Dept. of Child Welfare, or person or agency designated by it or Court
Louisiana	Yes	Dept. of Public Welfare
Maine	Yes (unless child is blood relative of one of petitioners or given for adoption by Dept. of Health and Welfare or licensed adoption agency); (may be waived by Court)	Dept. of Health and Welfare or licensed adoption agency

Chart F (Continued)

STATE	Is Investigation Required?	Who Must Make?
Maryland	Yes (unless agency adoption, or Court has personal knowledge)	Dept. of Public Welfare, licensed agency, probation officer or other person designated by Court
Massachusetts	Yes (if child under 14 and adoption not sponsored by agency)	Dept. of Public Welfare
Michigan	Yes	County agent, placement agency licensed by state, Michigan Children's Institute, State Dept. of Social Welfare, or county Social Welfare Board
Minnesota	Yes (may be waived by Court)	Commissioner of Public Welfare; any person, officer, or home designated by Court
Mississippi	Yes	Division of Welfare of State
Missouri	Yes	Dept. of Public Health and Welfare, any child-placement agency, juvenile court officer or other suitable person appointed by Court
Montana	Yes (in Court's discretion)	Division of Child Welfare
Nebraska	Yes (if Court deems advisable)	Board of Control or any child-placement agency licensed or approved by it
Nevada	Yes (Court may waive where a petitioner or spouse related to child within third degree)	Welfare Division of Dept. of Health and Welfare

New Hampshire	Yes (unless petitioner is natural mother)	Dept. of Public Welfare (where child placed for adoption by New Hampshire Children's Aid Society or New Hampshire Catholic Charities, Inc., Court may refer thereto for investigation)
New Jersey	Yes (usually)	Approved agency having principal office in New Jersey
New Mexico	Yes	New Mexico Dept. of Public Welfare
New York	Yes	Qualified disinterested person or authorized agency
North Carolina	Yes	County Superintendent of Public Welfare or authorized agency
North Dakota	Yes (Court may waive in exceptional cases)	Division of Child Welfare of Public Welfare Board
Ohio	Yes	"next friend"
Oklahoma	Yes (except when child is natural or adopted child of either petitioner)	Agency with custody or legal guardianship; otherwise state Dept. of Public Welfare or person qualified by training or experience designated by Court
Oregon	Yes	State Public Welfare Commission

Chart F (Continued)

STATE	Is Investigation Required?	Who Must Make?
Pennsylvania	Yes	A local public or consenting private child-care agency, State Dept. of Public Welfare, or appropriate person designated by Ct. (Ct. may accept the placing agency report in lieu)
Puerto Rico	Yes	A government public welfare agency
Rhode Island	Yes (except certain relative adoptions)	Dept. of Social Welfare: in child-placement agency adoptions, Ct. may accept case summary of agency instead; non-relative bringing or causing child to be brought into state for adoption must report to Division of Child Welfare Services within 45 days (latter investigates)
Tennessee	Yes	County Director of Public Welfare or licensed placement agency
Texas	Yes	Suitable person selected by court; Dept. of Public Welfare may investigate in any case not involving licensed agency placement
Utah	Yes (unless licensed placement agency's consent is filed or petitioner is spouse of natural parent)	Dept. of Public Welfare
Vermont	Yes (Court may waive in adoption of minor)	Dept. of Social Welfare (or licensed placement agency designated by it) (Dept. may waive on court's request)

Virginia	Yes	Commissioner of Public Welfare, or, in Ct.'s discretion, agency which placed child; on Commissioner's request, a local superintendent or other welfare agency of a county or city or agency that placed child must make the investigation
Washington	Yes	Approved agency, qualified salaried court employee, or other suitable and proper person
West Virginia	Yes	Suitable person or agency designated by court
Wisconsin	Yes	State Dept. of Public Welfare, licensed child-welfare agency or a county welfare dept. or children's board (investigation not required when guardian required to make recommendation files favorable one and said guardian is either Dept. of Public Welfare, licensed child-welfare agency, county welfare dept. or children's board)
Wyoming	Yes	Dept. of Public Welfare or private agency appointed by Ct. (in court's discretion)

Hearing

After notice has been given to the proper parties and the investigation has been made, a hearing must be held by the court. Frequently the hearing is in closed court or in the judge's chambers. At this time the court considers all the available information in order to determine whether or not the contemplated adoption is a proper one. The prospective adopters must ordinarily be present, as well as the child, if old enough to give consent. The court examines the interested parties, and, where an investigation has been made, considers the report thereof. Although the court usually is not bound by the recommendation of the report, the latter carries great weight and it is rare for a court to approve an adoption when the investigating agency's recommendation is unfavorable. The court may also hear witnesses and generally conduct a comprehensive hearing in order to satisfy itself as to the advisability of the adoption. Finally, if satisfied that the proposed adoption is in the best interests of the child, the court may make an order awarding the child to the adopting parents (as to the nature of this order, see Chapter 8). If not so satisfied, the court may adjourn the hearing to a later date in order to obtain further information or may reject the petition altogether and return the child to the persons or agency having custody prior to the proceeding. In all instances, the court's primary concern is the welfare and best interests of the child.

Chapter 8

ISSUING DECREE

After the hearing, the court—if approving the adoption—issues an order or decree. The nature of the decree depends upon the particular state law. In general it will be either:

1. A final decree, or
2. An interlocutory (temporary) decree.

Interlocutory Decree

An interlocutory decree is a **temporary** as opposed to a final decree. Its effect is that, at a later date—usually six months or a year—the court again considers the application. During the intervening period the child lives in the home of the prospective adopters. Ordinarily there is concomitant supervision by a licensed agency or by the State Welfare Board or equivalent department. The agency or board visits the adopting home to ascertain how the child is getting along, whether he is happy, and whether he is being properly cared for. If there has been an investigation prior to the hearing (see Chapter 7), the person or agency which made it usually will be designated to investigate and supervise during the trial period following issuance of the interlocutory decree.

In most states where interlocutory decrees are prescribed it is provided by statute that they may be revoked by the court at any time during the trial period. Such revocation may be either on the court's own motion or on application of either the natural or adopting parents, or possibly of the supervisory agency or other interested persons. When such an application is made, the court holds a hearing to determine its merits. Such applications, however, are relatively unusual.

Final Decree

If, as is most commonly the case, all goes well during the trial period, the court then issues a final decree approving the adoption (in some states, of course, there is only one (final) decree). The legal effect of a final decree of adoption is considered in the following chapter.

Child's Residence in Home of Petitioners

The following chart (Chart G) indicates that more than one-half of the states have no provision for an interlocutory decree. In such jurisdictions, as already observed, the original order is final and the adoption proceeding complete.

As noted earlier, the purpose of the interlocutory decree is to interpose a trial period to determine the compatability of the parties and to ascertain whether the welfare and happiness of all concerned will best be served by approval of the petition. Even states having no interlocutory decrees usually provide for a similar trial period in some other manner. This usually takes the form of a requirement that the child must have lived in the petitioners' home for a specified period before approval of the petition, although the court is often authorized, in its discretion, to either waive this requirement or shorten the otherwise specified period. This practice, however, is ordinarily not as effective in protecting the child's interests as is the interlocutory decree. For one thing, the preliminary period of residence is frequently unsupervised (a requirement incident to interlocutory decrees in most states).

It should again be noted that in agency adoptions, the agency requirements may be actually more stringent than those imposed by statute. Virtually all such agencies require that the child live with the prospective adopters for a specified period (usually one year) before the agency will approve the adoption. This, of course, affords additional protection to all concerned.

Chart G classifies the states with respect to the practice of requiring interlocutory decrees, the periods of time intervening before issuance of final decrees, and the requirements respecting investigation or supervision during these periods. The chart also indicates whether other trial residence requirements are provided in place of an interlocutory decree. It will be seen that in a few states both types of provisions obtain.

Chart G

INTERLOCUTORY DECREES AND TRIAL RESIDENCE REQUIREMENTS

STATE	Interlocutory Decree?	Period Before Final Order	Intervening Supervision?	Other Trial Residence Required?	How Long?
Alabama	Yes	Six months	Yes	No	
Alaska	No			No	
Arizona	Yes	One year		No	
Arkansas	Yes	Six months	Yes	No	
California	No			No	
Colorado	Yes(4)	One year or shorter period determined by court		No	
Connecticut	Yes(4)	12-13 months from application		No	
Delaware	No		Yes	Yes	One year (may be reduced to six months)

Chart G (Continued)

STATE	Interlocutory Decree?	Period Before Final Order	Intervening Supervision?	Other Trial Residence Required?	How Long?
District of Columbia	Yes(4)	Six months	Yes	Yes	Six months
Florida	No			Yes	Petition heard after 90 days residence under supervision of Welfare Board (with certain exceptions)
Georgia	No			No	
Hawaii	No(*)			No	
Idaho	No			No	
Illinois	Yes	Six months		Yes	Six months
Indiana	No		By approved agency for period set by court		

State					
Iowa	No			Yes	12 months (court may shorten or waive)
Kansas	No			No	
Kentucky	No			Yes	Three months just before petition
Louisiana	Yes	At least six months	At least twice	Yes	One year
Maine	No		Court may require supervision	Yes	One year (in Ct.'s discretion)
Maryland	Yes (in Ct.'s discretion)		Not more than one year	No	
Massachusetts	No			Yes	One year (Ct. may waive for cause)
Michigan	Yes	One year (Ct. may waive in best interests of child unless adopters object in writing)	Yes	No	

Chart G (Continued)

STATE	Interlocutory Decree?	Period Before Final Order	Intervening Supervision?	Other Trial Residence Required?	How Long?
Minnesota	No			Yes	Six months (Ct. may waive)
Mississippi	Yes	Six months (except in adoption of step-child or child related within third degree or any case where chancellor deems it unnecessary; period may also be shortened by time child in adopters' home before interlocutory decree)		No	
Missouri	No			Yes	Nine months

State					
Montana	Yes	Six months (in step-child or blood relative adoptions, or if court finds it in child's best interests, court may, after examining investigative report, waive interlocutory decree and six months period and grant final decree)		No	
Nebraska	No			Yes	Six months immediately preceding decree
Nevada	No			Yes	Six months
New Hampshire	Yes	One year or shorter period determined by court	Yes	No	
New Jersey	No (agency adoption) Yes (otherwise, ex-	One year (if adoptee	Yes	Yes	Six months

Chart G (Continued)

STATE	Interlocutory Decree?	Period Before Final Order	Intervening Supervision?	Other Trial Residence Required?	How Long?
New Jersey (cont'd)	cept where adopter is brother, sister, aunt, uncle, grandparent, stepparent (Ct. may waive)	lived with adopter continuously since before Jan. 1. 1954. period may be less)			
New Mexico	No			Yes	Six mos. (if child under one year, until that age is reached) (on motion, and for good cause shown, or where petitioner is non-resident, Ct. may make such residence requirements as may be convenient and proper)

State				
New York	No		Yes	Six months (child under 18, but Ct. may waive)
North Carolina	Yes(1)	One year (2)	Yes	One year (1) (2)
North Dakota	No		Yes	Six months (may be waived by Ct.)
Ohio	Yes (except in step-child adoptions or where child placed in adopter's home six months under agency supervision)	Six months	Yes	Six months
Oklahoma	Yes (waivable in stepchild adoption where child living in petitioners' home, or agency adoptions where child in home six months just before hearing, visited at reasonable inter-	Six months	No	

Chart G (Continued)

STATE	Interlocutory Decree?	Period Before Final Order	Intervening Supervision?	Other Trial Residence Required?	How Long?
Oklahoma (cont'd)	vals by agency and agency recommends the adoption)				
Oregon	No			No	
Pennsylvania	No			Yes	Six months (except relative adoption)
Puerto Rico	Yes	Six months	Yes	No	
Rhode Island	No			Yes	Six months (waivable by Ct. for good cause)
South Carolina	Yes	Six months (interlocutory decree and waiting period waivable by Ct. in stepchild or relative adoptions or in best interests of child)	Yes	No	

State					
South Dakota	No			Yes	Six months
Tennessee	Yes	One year from interlocutory decree and within two years of filing petition(3)	Yes	No	
Texas	No			Yes	Six months (Ct. may waive)
Utah	No			Yes	One year
Vermont	No			Yes	Six months (Ct. may certify as unnecessary)
Virginia	Yes	Six months (except agency adoptions where child in petitioners' home six months and visited three times, or where child 12 yrs. old and and in home five years)		Yes	Six months (Dept. of Public Welfare may recommend immediate hearing)
Washington	Yes	Six months		No	

Chart G (Continued)

STATE	Interlocutory Decree?	Period Before Final Order	Intervening Supervision?	Other Trial Residence Required?	How Long?
West Virginia	No			Yes	Six months
Wisconsin	No			Yes	Six months (unless petitioner is step-parent or blood relative, or guardian's approval filed)
Wyoming	Yes	Six months		Yes	Six months

(1) May be waived if child is 6 years old and has lived with the petitioners at least five years.
(2) In placement agency adoptions, may deduct time child has been in petitioners' home.
(3) Court may waive in adoptions of stepchild, grandchild, nephew or niece, or if child in petitioners' home for more than one year before filing of the petition.
(4) In court's discretion.
(*) Court *may* postpone effective date of final decree until six months after it is rendered.

Annulment of Final Order

As noted in the preceding text, in states having interlocutory decrees, such decrees may be revoked at any time before issuance of a final decree. Once a final order has issued, however, the proceeding is complete and the case closed. The adoptee is now legally the child of the adopting parents for all purposes. Nevertheless, under certain exceptional circumstances, a proceeding may later be brought to annul the final order. In some states, the order may be annuled if the adopting parents have not discharged their duty to the child properly, while in some the adopting parents may seek an annulment if the child develops a disease from a preexisting condition not known at the time of adoption. In many states an action to annul may be brought only within a relatively short period of time following the final decree. In a few jurisdictions a child adopted as a minor has the option of applying for an annulment upon reaching the age of 21. As already indicated, provisions for annulment cover cases attended by unusual circumstances. The essential element to bear in mind is that, in the typical case, an adoption proceeding is consummated upon entry of the final decree, whereafter the adoptee is, for legal purposes, the child of the adopters.

Chapter 9

ADOPTION AND ITS LEGAL EFFECTS

As noted at the outset of the text, the general effect of an adoption decree is the termination of rights and duties between the child and its natural parents and substitution of an equivalent status between the child and its adoptive parents. Some statutes go into greater detail and specify that the child shall be entitled to education, care and maintenance by the adopting parents. These obligations, of course, devolve naturally upon the adopting parents even though no such specific statutory requirements are set forth. In fact, it may be taken as a general rule that, unless specific exceptions are provided by law, the effect of adoption is to establish as between the adoptive parents and the child all the rights and duties as normally exist between the child and its natural parents.

Change of Name

Practically all states permit change of the child's surname to that of its adoptive parents. If such a change is desired, the adoption petition should specifically request the inclusion in the forthcoming decree of such a provision. For example, see the form of petition set forth in Chapter 5.

Records; Birth Certificate

Practically all states now provide for making adoption proceeding records secret and available for inspection only by court order.

In most states it is possible to obtain the issuance of a new birth certificate reciting the new name of the adopted child. The certificate will not reveal any information about the natural parents or otherwise show that the child has been adopted. Generaly, the old certificate will be sealed and filed, and can only be opened on request of the adopted person, if of legal age, or by an order of the court.

Inheritance

Undoubtedly the most troublesome question arising after adoption is that of inheritance. As a general rule the child may inherit from the adopting parents and this is provided for specifically in practically all statutes. However, a few states restrict the child's right of inheritance by not permitting it to take property expressly limited to heirs of the body. Some of the states having provisions of this character are Maine, Ohio, Vermont and West Virginia.

Ordinarily, too, the adopting parents may inherit from the child, but, again, a few states have contrary rules. In Georgia, for example, the adopting parents cannot inherit property acquired or inherited by the child from blood relatives. In Tennessee adoptive parents may inherit property acquired by the adoptee after adoption. In Arkansas the adoptive parents do not inherit property received from the natural parents and the same rule applies in Massachusetts.

The question frequently arises as to whether or not the child may still inherit from its natural parents. In light of the rule that adoption terminates all legal relationships between them, the general rule is that, in the absence of specific statutory provision, the child may not so inherit. However, a number of states have such provisions in their statutes. Included among these are Alabama, Arkansas, Florida, Maine, Massachusetts, Michigan, Texas, Vermont and West Virginia. In some states—Iowa for example—even in the absence of specific statute, the courts have held that the child may inherit from its natural parents under common law. In a number of states, although the child may inherit from its natural parents, they may not inherit from the child. In many states the substituted relationship obtains for all purposes, including the right of inheritance.

Extremely complicated issues may arise regarding the relationship for purposes of inheritance between the adopted child and other relatives of the adoptive parents. For example, may the adopted child inherit from his "sisters" and "brothers" who are the natural children of the adopters? The general rule seems to be that a statute making the adopted child the heir of the adopting parents does not entitle it to claim as heir of the adopter's relatives. In some states this rule has been modified either by statute or judicial pronouncement. The subject is extremely complicated and the law so diverse among the several states that it is impossible to give categorical answers to such questions without first knowing all the facts and circumstances of the particular case.

Citizenship

An alien child adopted by an American citizen does not automatically acquire citizenship, but remains an alien until naturalized. The applicable statute-8 USCA 1434-provides that an adopted child is required to establish two years residence in the United States prior to the filing of a petition for naturalization.

A subsection to the above cited statute was added in 1957. As amended in 1958, this subsection now provides as follows:

"(c) Any such adopted child(1) one of whose adoptive parents is (A) a citizen of the United States, (B) in the Armed Forces of the United States or in the employment of the Government of the United States, or of an American institution of research recognized as such by the Attorney General, or of an American firm or corporation engaged in whole or in part in the development of foreign trade and commerce of the United States, or a subsidiary thereof, or of a public international organization in which the United States participates by treaty or statute or is authorized to perform the ministerial or priestly functions of a religious denomination having a bona fide organization within the United States, or is engaged solely as a missionary by a religious denomination or by an international mission organization having a bona fide organization within the United States, and (C) regularly stationed abroad in such service or employment, and (2) who is in the United States at the time of naturalization, and (3) whose citizen adoptive parent declares before the naturalization court in good faith an intention to have such child take up residence within the United States immediately upon the termination of such service or employment abroad of such citizen adoptive parent, may be naturalized upon the compliance with all the requirements of the naturalization laws except that no prior residence or specified period of physical presence within the United States or within the jurisdiction of the naturalization court or proof thereof shall be required, and paragraph (3) of subsection (a) of this section shall not be applicable."*

*The subsection mentioned provides as follows: "subsequent to such adoption has resided continuously in the United States in legal custody of the adoptive parents or parents for two years prior to the date of filing such petition."

To bring the adopted child into the country, approval of the United States Immigration Service must be obtained. The investigation into the adopting couple's background is thorough and if the Immigration Service is dissatisfied with what it finds or with the report on the health of the child which must be submitted, the child will not be admitted to the United States.

A lawyer should be consulted before leaving this country to adopt abroad. Among other things, the lawyer can make sure a couple have the complete documentation necessary before leaving the country.

Chapter 10

FOREIGN ADOPTIONS

There are two adoptive routes to choose from in making an adoption of a foreign child, the same two as are available in domestic adoptions: agencies or individuals.

Adoptions can be made through an agency licensed to arrange adoptions in specific foreign countries. Most such agencies are also licensed by a state in the United States.

Some countries permit legal adoptions to be arranged by private individuals. For the most part, the same problems that exist with private adoptions in the United States can take place with independent adoptions abroad. On the other hand, private contacts are predominantly the rule in the following countries: Brazil, Cambodia, Costa Rica, El Salvador, Haiti, Honduras, Indonesia, Laos, Lebanon, Mexico, Nepal, Peru, and Thailand.

The major sources of information about independent contacts are the Foreign Adoption Center in Boulder, Colorado, and local adoptive parents groups.

A couple must either go abroad themselves to adopt a child or meet the preadoptive requirements of the state in which they live. They will be investigated by the court or by the social welfare department or by a private adoption agency and if approved are authorized to bring a child into this country for adoption.

Foreign adoptions made by couples who go abroad and remain for a short time in the country in which they adopt have a fundamental security. There is no six-months' or year-long suspense as the adoptive couple worry about whether the mother may change her mind or some complication developes. The adoption is completed immediately, and the adopting parents return to the United States secure in the final decree. Since they go to a foreign country, the chance of any possible future claim to the child surviving the complications of international law is also nonexistent.

68

GLOSSARY

Abandoned child — According to New York State Law, a child under sixteen years of age left destitute, "or without proper food, shelter, or clothes, or without being visited or having payments made toward his support, for a period of at least one year, by his parents... without good reason."

Adoption — Becoming a parent through a legal and social process rather than through a biological one.

Adoption Exchange — (NYSAE) A State-administered referral service to increase adoption opportunities for potential families and available children. State law mandates registration of all legally free children who have been waiting for at least six months for an adoptive home as well as any agency-approved families for whom a child could not be found within six months of the approval.

Adoptive discharge — A child who has been placed in an adoptive home and subsequently legally adopted through the court, at which time he is discharged from foster care.

Adoptive parent organization — A group of interested people, often past or prospective adoptive parents, to promote interest in adoption, particularly of "hard-to-place" children.

Adoptive placement — The placing of an available child in a home with a definite expectation that he will be legally adopted.

Agency placement — An adoptive placement arranged by a public or voluntary agency licensed by the state Board of Social Welfare.

ALMA — (Adoptees' Liberty Movement Association)- A group of adults who were adopted as children and are committed to the repeal of restriction of adoption records.

ARENA — (Adoption Resource Exchange of North America) - An adoption referral service that operates under the auspices of the Child Welfare League of America and includes children and families from throughout the United States and Canada.

CAP Book — A multiple listing service of photographs and summaries describing many of the children in New York State who are in need of adoption that is operated by an adoptive parent organization, the Council of Adoptive Parents (CAP) of Rochester, and funded by the Department.

Foster Care — Substitute care of a child by someone other than the natural parents, relatives within the second degree or legal guardian which is arranged for and supervised by an authorized social service agency.

Independent adoptive placement — Adoptive placement arranged directly by the parent, legal guardian or relative within the second degree rather than placement by an agency.

Neglected child — According to State Law, a boy under sixteen years of age or a girl less than eighteen whose parent does not provide adequately for him though financially able to do so, or who is likely to suffer from improper guardianship or who has been deserted by his parent or guardian.

Private agency — See Voluntary Child Caring Organization.

Public agency — A public facility which is operated in this State by the local department of social services.

Subsidized adoption — An adoption for which public funds for support of a child who has been or is in the process of being legally adopted.

Voluntary child caring organization — Private organization that provides foster care and/or adoption services—usually for a large number of children—under a license from the State Board of Social Welfare.

"Waiting" child — A child who is still waiting for a permanent home, perhaps because he has been classified "hard-to-place" as a result of his age or race, or a physical or mental handicap.

71

Appendix A

RECENT COURT CASES ON ADOPTION ISSUES

In New York State

Fitzsimmons vs. Liuni (concluded 1967). The Liuni family had cared for a foster child, Beth, from the age of five days and she had become very much part of the family by the time Ulster County Department of Social Services wanted to remove her to place in an adoptive home at age 3½. The foster parents had wanted to adopt her themselves but were denied the right. At the habeas corpus proceeding, the Social Services Commissioner and his staff explained that adoption practice was a "scientific process," involving the careful matching of child and parents, for ethnic and national background, eye and hair coloring, intellectual ability and so on. The Liunis were also considered inappropriate for adopting parents because they were too old and they had other children—the policy was to place adoptive children with childless couples under 35 years of age. The Liunis refused to give the child up because they felt, and were supported by a child psychiatrist, that it would be very unlikely for her to be moved to a new family without long term, perhaps permanent, emotional harm.

The Family Court judge decided that the Liunis should return the child to the County. This decision was made to avoid the permanent foster care which would result since the Social Services Commissioner's consent was necessary, but not unlikely, before an adoption could be consummated.

Representative Joseph Y. Resnick, whose district included Ulster County, took the story to the news media, thereby drawing much public attention to the case. He charged the Judge with conflict of interest since his wife was the Commissioner's first counsin. A panel of judges ruled that a new hearing with a different family court judge was in order.

The commissioner finally bowed to the pressure of the massive public protest which resulted, withdrew the habeas corpus petition, and agreed to consent to the adoption of the child by the Liunis, which the newly-assigned family court judge signed.

72

As a result of this case, new laws were passed to give rights and preference in adoption to foster parents after caring for a child for more than two years.

In 1971, there were two cases decided relating to religious matching in adoption: the *Matter of Maxwell* and *Dickens vs. Ernesto.*

The *Matter of Maxwell* involved an adoption of a Catholic child placed with a Protestant-Jewish couple. According to the law, a child must be placed "when practicable" with parents of the same religion. The Maxwell case, however, stated that "religious matching of the child and the adoptive parents cannot be deemed 'practicable'... if the matching effort will be detrimental to the child's psychic and emotional welfare." The court pointed out that it was important for a child to be placed early to have a stable environment in infancy to assure his development; delay to secure religious matching must be considered detrimental.

The *Dickens vs. Ernesto* case arose from the refusal of an application to adopt because the petitioners lacked religious affiliation. The proceeding claimed that the religious affiliation requirements of the law which provided for the "establishment of religion," was unconstitutional. The court ruled that nothing in the laws required denial based on absence of religion but only that placement when practicable be with persons of the same religion as the child. Children whose religion is unknown are to be placed in good homes with the best temporal interests of the child in mind regardless of the religion or lack of religion of the family. Since the law only requires religious matching "when practicable," it is not unconstitutional.

Decisions in cases in 1971 upheld the superior right of the mother, thereby causing legislators to revise the laws relating to surrender and consent.

In *Ferro vs. Bacile* the prospective adoptive parents lost the child to the natural mother who had consented to a private placement adoption shortly after the child's birth. Fourteen months later the mother began legal proceedings to have the child returned to her. At the time of her consent her parents had pressured her to give up the child but, because of her subsequent marriage, the natural mother felt she could make a home for her son. Despite testimony from doctors that return of the child would be detrimental, the courts upheld the right of the natural mother and removed the three-year-old boy from his adoptive home.

Scarpetta vs. Spence-Chapin Adoption Service, publicized widely as the "Baby Lenore" case was a case in which the natural mother decided to revoke the surrender of her child. When a New York State court ordered the return of the child to her natural mother, the adoption family fled to Miami where the courts judged the child's interest would best be served by her adopting parents. The public controversy over this case lead to amendments in the law which provide for a period of only thirty days during which a mother can revoke her surrender and for a requirement that agencies inform adopting parents of any such proceedings immediately.

Spence-Chapin vs. Polk was a slightly different case in that the agency and the natural mother both brought legal proceedings against the foster parents who desired to adopt the child. The child had been placed with the foster family when she was five months old. The family requested that they be allowed to adopt the child and the caseworker recommended to her agency that they be permitted to adopt once the surrender was obtained. When the natural mother signed the surrender, she requested that the child be placed with a Chinese family since both of the natural parents were Chinese. The agency's committee responsible for adoptive placement refused permission to the foster parents on the basis that they were too old, had five natural children, and were not Chinese. It was felt by the agency, and later by the courts, that the child might suffer later identity problems because of the racial difference between the child and the Caucasian family living in a Caucasian community.

Although the agency began the first habeas corpus proceedings against the foster family, the mother later began one of her own upon learning the child was not placed with a Chinese family. Meanwhile, she made a plan for the child which was approved by both the agency and the Social Services Commissioner. The court ruled that only the commissioner's consent is necessary to reverse the surrender and give the mother custody of the child.

The judge, therefore, ruled that "identity problems that might arise from the racial difference . . . outweigh the immediate anxiety that might be caused by separation from foster parents now." In its decision the court cited "the best interests of the child and the superior right of the natural mother."

The rights of unmarried fathers were raised in 1972 in the *Stanley vs. Illinois* case, which was finally decided in the United States Supreme Court. The petitioner claimed that he did not receive equal protection of the law because his children were taken from him without a hearing establishing unfitness. Under Illinois law such a hearing is required before custody is denied of children of married or divorced parents and unmarried mothers. The Supreme Court found the presumption of the Illinois law that all unmarried fathers are unfit is conflicts with due process of the law and denies such fathers equal protection of the law. The response to this case and others has been legislation in a few states to give some type of notice to putative fathers prior to adoption; New York is one of these states. The child Welfare League recommends obtaining consent, a waiver, or a denial of paternity from putative fathers to prevent later litigation that might delay adoption proceedings.

Other Jurisdictions

In a second case, Lewis-Rothstein, an unwed mother terminated her parental rights to her child without telling the child's bio father, who was denied a hearing on his termination of parental rights. This case also was referred to the Supreme Court but remanded back to the Wisconsin Supreme Court with orders to reconsider its first decision that the unwed father had no rights to a hearing in view of the Stanley case recommendations. It also was suggested that in cases arising after April 4, 1972, and the alleged bio fathers were not advised at the time that they had any rights. If the courts find that these rights were violated and bio fathers have the right to a hearing, under current practices they must be declared legally the child's bio father and be shown fit to raise the child. During this time, the bio mother often can make a reconsideration of her prior termination and make a claim for parental rights. But if the current trend holds, the well-being of the child will be the primary consideration.

Adoptions made before April 4, 1972, would not be affected and most adoption judges are being meticulous about correct procedures in current cases to avoid future challenges. There has been a legal defense fund established to help parents involved in custody challenges by the Open Door Society of Milwaukee, Wisconsin.

A 1973 California case held that prospective adoptive parents involved with the placement of a child for adoption have the right to a hearing on a change in their status by a placement agency. Parents also are entitled to notice prior to proposed termination of placement, except in extraordinary cases where there is danger to the child's health and safety.

Appendix B

UNIFORM ADOPTION ACT

1969 REVISED ACT
Amended 1971

§ 1. [Definitions]

As used in this Act, unless the context otherwise requires.

(1) "child" means a son or daughter, whether by birth or by adoption;

(2) "Court" means the [here insert name of the court or branch]

77

court of this State, and when the context requires means of court of any other state empowered to grant petitions for adoption;

(3) "minor" means [a male] [an individual] under the age of [18] [21] years [and a female under the age of 18 years];

(4) "adult" means an individual who is not a minor;

(5) "agency" means any peson certified, licensed, or otherwise specially empowered by law or rule to place minors for adoption;

(6) "person" means an individual, corporation, government or governmental subdivision or agency, business trust, estate, trust, partnership or association, or any other legal entity.

Commissioners' Note

"Child" is defined so as to include both an adult and a minor as a child capable of being adopted. If an adult is adopted, he becomes a "child" of the adoptive parents to the same extent that a natural child is a "child" of his natural parents even though he is an adult.

The definition of "minor" is the more important definition of this Act. The original Uniform Adoption Act accepted the then general definition of minority. It is well known that many variations have developed in state law as to the age attached to minority in relation to particular purposes. The voting age, the drinking age, the age of consent, and the like now vary considerbly in the states. The pamphlet "Legislative Guides for the Termination of Parental Rights and Responsibilities and the Adoption of Children" prepared by the Children's Bureau of the United States Department of Health, Education and Welfare in 1957 and

again in 1961 uses as the age for a "minnor" the age of 18 whether a male or female. The two matters as to which the definition is important in this Act are the age of the adopted person for whom the natural parents must consent to his adoption and the age of a parent who may consent to the adoption of his own child. When the question is whether the child to be adopted must also consent, a different age is proposed in this Act. See section 10.

The definition of "person" is taken from the Uniform Statutory Construction Act and is broad enough to include both a public social welfare agency or an independent social welfare agency. It is also broad enough to include a natural person acting to place children for adoption, but such a person may act as a placing agency only if he is "certified, licensed or otherwise empowered to place children for adoption."

Action in Adopting Jurisdictions

Variations from Official Text:

North Dakota. Defines "minor" as
an individual under the age of eighteen years.

§ 2. [Who May Be Adopted]

Any individual may be adopted.

Commissioners' Note

This section is intended to permit
the combination in one act of
provisions for adotion of minors
and provisions for the adoption of
adults. Either a minor or an adult
may be adopted. This Act provides,
in certain places, for a different
procedure when an adult is to be
adopted from that provided when a
minor is to be adopted.

§ 3. [Who May Adopt]

The following individuals may adopt:

(1) a husband and wife together although one or both are minors;

(2) an unmarried adult;

(3) the unmarried father or mother of the individual to be
adopted;

(4) a married individual without the other spouse jointing as a
petitioner, if the individual to be adopted is not his spouse, and if

(i) the other spouse is a parent of the individual to be adopted
and consents to the adoption;
(ii) the petitioner and the other spouse are legally separated; or
(iii) the failure of the other spouse to join in the petition or to
consent to the adoption is excused by the Court by reason of
prolonged unexplained absence, unavailability, incapacity, or
circumstances constituting an unreasonable withholding of
consent.

Commissioners' Note

This section clarifies the list of
persons entitled to adopt a child. In
subsection (1) a husband and wife
acting together are entitled to adopt
even though one or both of them is
a "minor," that is, under the age of

79

contracting as provided in this act or in general law. The Act lists several cases where a married person may adopt a child without the other spouse joining as petitioner and it lists one situation in which an individual may not be adopted—where the individual is a spouse of the petitioner. The Act permits an adult unmarried person to adopt a child; it permits any unmarried father or mother to adopt his own child; and it permits a married individual without the other spouse joining as a petitioner to adopt an individual if the other spouse is a parent of the person to be adopted and consents to the adoption or the petitioner and the other spouse are legally separated; or the nonjoining spouse is excused from participation by the court by reason of circumstances constituting an unreasonable withholding of consent. Thus, a married individual whose spouse is a missing person or is incapacitated may adopt an individual without the consent of the other spouse.

In adoption proceedings commenced after placement of the child by an agency, it is contemplated that before the petition for adoption has been filed, that either relinquishment of the right to consent or a court order terminating parental rights under section 19 will have occurred, so that the consent of the natural parent is not required in the adoption proceedings. The person whose consent may be dispensed with are listed in section 6.

Parental consent is required only where the person to be adopted is a minor child as that term is defined in section 1. If the person to be adopted is an adult or if the person to be adopted is married whether or not he be an adult, the consent of the spouse of the person to be adopted is required.

Subdivision (2) of subsection (a) requires consent of the father of the minor who married the mother after the minor was conceived and who was divorced from the mother before the minor was born. It also requires the father to have a relationship to the child amounting to more than a mere acknowledgment or determination of paternity before his consent is required. Modern casses hold that the "putative father has no parental rights and no right to notice of any hearing prior to such [voluntary termination of parental rights by the natural mother] proceedings. See State ex rel. Lewis et al. v. Lutheran Social Services of Wisconsin and Upper Michigan (Wis. 1970) 178 N.W. 2d 56, and In re Brennan, 270 Nubb, 455, 134 N. W. 2d 126.

Under the laws of many states, the natural father legitimates the child of an unwed mother by marriage to her or by receiving the child into his own home and publicly treating the child as his. The proposed Uniform Legitimacy Act, which has not yet been approved by the National Conference, will likely specify the circumstances under which consent of the unwed father to adoption is required. Accordingly, a state enacting the Revised Uniform Adoption Act should select the bracketed language that is appropriate at the time of enactment.

Subsection (a) (3) includes a father having custody of his illegitimate minor child, a legal guardian, or an agency authorized to place the child. If the legal guardian is not empowered to consent to the adoption of the minor child, the court having jurisdiction of the custody of the minor may consent in place of the guardian.

Subsection (a) (5) requires the consent of the person to be adopted if he is more than 10 years of age, but flexibility is introduced by permitting the court to dispense with his consent. Apparently, there are cases particularly of "stepchildren" in which the child does not know that he is a stepchild and in terms of his best interest, it would be better not to disclose to him at the time of the adoption proceedings that he is being adopted by a stepfather.

§ 4. [Venue, Inconvenient Forum, Caption]

(a) Proceedings for adoption must be brought in the Court for the place in which, at the time of filing or granting the petition, the petitioner or the individual to be adopted resides or is in military service or in which the agency having the care, custody, or control of the minor is located.

(b) If the Court finds in the interest of substantial justice that the matter should be heard in another forum, the Court may [transfer,] stay or dismiss the proceeding in whole or in part on any conditions that are just.

(c) The caption of a petition for adoption shall be styled substantially "In the Matter of the Adoption of _____." The person to be adopted shall be designated in the caption under the name by which he is to be known if the petition is granted. If the child is placed for adoption by an agency, any name by which the child was previously known shall not be disclosed in the petition, the notice of hearing, or in the decree of adoption.

Commissioners' Note

The name of the appropriate court or division of the court should be inserted in subsection (a) and again in subsection (b).

Jurisdiction is based on residence of either the person seeking to adopt the child or the residence of the child at the time of adoption. The section thus permits the parents to bring the adoption action in the court of the place where the agency making the placement is located. If the placement is "an independent placement" or by an agency in another state, the petitioners may bring the proceeding in the place of their own residence if they have resided in the state for 6 months preceding the filing of the petition.

Subsection (b) is taken from the Uniform Interstate and International Procedure Act.

§ 5. [Persons Required to Consent to Adoption]

(a) Unless consent is not required under section 6, a petition to adopt a minor may be granted only if written consent to a particular adoption has been executed by:

> (1) the mother of the minor;

> (2) the father of the minor if the father was married to the mother at the time the minor was conceived or at any time thereafter, the minor is his child by adotion, or [he has otherwise legitimated the minor according to the laws of the place in which the adoption proceeding is brought] [his consent is required under the Uniform Legitimacy Act];

> (3) any person lawfully entitled to custody of the minor or empowered to consent;

> (4) the court having jurisdiction to determine custody of the minor, if the legal guardian or custodian of the person of the minor is not empowered to consent to the adoption;

> (5) the minor, if more than [10] years of age, unless the Court in the best interest of the minor dispenses with the minor's consent; and

> (6) the spouse of the minor to be adopted.

(b) A petition to adopt an adult may be granted only if written consent to adoption has been executed by the adult and the adult's spouse.

§ 6. [Persons as to Whom Consent and Notice Not Required]

(a) Consent to adoption is not required of:

> (1) a parent who has [deserted a child without affording means of identification, or who has] abandoned a child;

(2) a parent of a child in the custody of another, if the parent for a period of at least one year has failed significantly without justifiable cause (i) to communicate with the child or (ii) to provide for the care and support of the child as required by law or judicial decree;

(3) the father of a minor if the father's consent is not required by section 5(a) (2);

(4) a parent who has relinquished his right to consent under section 19;

(5) a parent whose parental rights have been terminated by order of court under section 19;

(6) a parent judicially declared incompetent or mentally defective if the Court dispenses with the parent's consent;

(7) any parent of the individual to be adopted, if (i) the individual is a minor [18] or more years of age and the Court dispenses with the consent of the parent or (ii) the individual is an adult;

(8) any legal guardian or lawful custodian of the individual to be adopted, other than a parent, who has failed to respond in writing to a request for consent for a period of [60] days or who, after examination of his written reasons for withholding consent, is found by the Court to be withholding his consent unreasonably; or

(9) the spouse of the individual to be adopted, if the failure of the spouse to consent to the adoption is excused by the Court by reason of prolonged unexplained absence, unavailability, incapacity, or circumstances constituting an unreasonable withholding of consent.

(b) Except as provided in section 11, notice of a hearing on a petition for adoption need not be given to a person whose consent is not required or to a person whose consent or relinquishment has been filed with the petition.

Commissioners' Note

This section deals primarily with legal excuses for not offering the consent of a parent or guardian. In an agency placement the excuse most likely will be that in subsections (a) (4) and (5) where prior to the proceeding the parent has relinquished his rights or the rights have been terminated under section 19 or other appropriate judicial proceedings.

Subsections (1) and (2) excuse termination of parental rights in a separate proceeding where the child has been abandoned or the parent has deserted the child. Subsection (a) (1) would require the court to find (after notice under section 11) that the child has been abandoned. If the evidence otherwise establishes the requisite intent, this fact may be found even after a relatively short time of desertion or abandonment. Subsection (a) (2) is designed to permit the court to find that consent to adoption is unnecessary without finding that the parent has "abandoned" the child by the

court finding the existence of certain facts of a prescribed duration. Failure to attempt to communicate with the child for 3 years "when the parent is able to do so" or failure to provide support for the child "when the parent is able to do so" for one year permit the court to find that the consent of the parent is unnecessary. The phrase "when able to do so" would permit the court to hold the subsection inapplicable if the failure to communicate or to provide support was due to the actions of the person having custody of the child preventing the parent from communicating or supporting the child.

If a state defines an adult in section 1 as an individual 18 or more years of age, subparagraph (7) (i) should be utilized only if the state chooses to authorize the adoption of an individual less than 18 years of age without parental consent and the Court dispenses with such consent.

Action in Adopting Jurisdictions

Variations from Official Text:
North Dakota. Subsec. (a)(7) reads: "Any parent of the individual to be adopted, if the individual is an adult."

§7. [How Consent is Executed]

(a) The required consent to adoption shall be executed at any time after the birth of the child and in the manner following:

    (1) if by the individual to be adopted, in the presence of the court;

(2) if by an agency, by the executive head or other authorized representative, in the presence of a person authorized to take acknowledgements;

(3) if by any other person, in the presence of the Court [or in the presence of a person authorized to take acknowledments];

(4) if by a court, by appropriate order or certificate.

(b) A consent which does not name or otherwise identify the adopting parent is valid if the consent [is executed in the presence of the Court and] contains a statement by the person whose consent it is that the person consenting voluntarily executed the consent irrespective of disclosure of the name or other identification of the adopting parent.

Commissioners' Note

This section is intended to prescribe the method by which consents may be executed. Consents executed "in the presence of the court" need no further formalities. Consents otherwise executed must be executed in the presence of a person authorized to take acknowledments. The method for executing a consent should be distinguished from the method for relinquishment of a right to consent which is prescribed in Section 19.

Subsection (b) is designed to clarify a point which seems to be ambiguous under some law as to whether the consent must be a consent to adoption by a particular individual. The subsection authorizes a consent "in blank" if the form of the consent contains a statement that a person consented voluntarily without disclosure of the name or other identification of the adopting parent.

The bracketing of language in subdivision (3) of subsection (a) and the addition of bracketed language in subsection (b) is provided for any state that wishes to follow the recommendation of the Council of the Section on Family Law of the American Bar Association that all consents to adoption by individuals should be executed in the presence of the Court. The Special Committee of the National Conference feels that such a procedural requirement is too severe and unnecessary.

Amendments

Subsec. (b) was amended in 1971 by addition of bracketed material.

§ 8. [Withdrawal of Consent]

(a) A consent to adoption cannot be withdrawn after the entry of a decree of adoption.

(b) A consent to adoption may be withdrawn prior to the entry of a decree of adoption if the Court finds, after notice and opportunity to be heard is afforded to petitioner, the person seeking the withdrawal, and the agency placing a child for adoption, that the withdrawal is in the best interest of the individual to be adopted and the Court orders the withdrawal.

Commissioners' Note

This section limits the opportunity of a person to withdraw his consent. No withdrawal is permitted after entry of an interlocutory or final decree of adoption. Withdrawal of consent before entry of the decree may be made only with the consent of the Court on the basis of a finding that withdrawal of consent is in the best interest of the child.

Action in Adopting Jurisdictions

Variations from Official Text:

Oklahoma. Sections reads: "Withdrawal of any consent filed in connection with a petition for adoption hereunder shall not be permitted, except that the court, after notice and opportunity to be heard is given to the petitioner by the person seeking to withdraw consent and notice to any agency participating in the adoption proceedings, may, if it finds that the best interest of the child will be furthered thereby, issue a written order permitting the withdrawal of such consent if request for leave to withdraw consent is submitted in writing not later than thirty (30) days after consent was executed. The entry of the interlocutory or final decree of adoption renders any consent irrevocable."

§ 9. [Petition for Adoption]

(a) A petition for adoption shall be signed and verified by the petitioner, filed with the clerk of the Court, and state:

(1) the date and place of birth of the individual to be adopted, if known;

(2) the name to be used for the individual to be adopted;

(3) the date [petitioner acquired custody of the minor and] of placement of the minor and the name of the person placing the minor;

(4) the full name, age, place and duration of residence of the petitioner;

(5) the marital status of the petitioner, including the date and place of marriage, if married;

(6) that the petitioner has facilities and resources, including those available under a subsidy agreement, suitable to provide for the nurture and care of the minor to be adopted, and that it is the desire of the petitioner to establish the relationship of parent and child with the individual to be adopted;

(7) a description and estimate of value of any property of the individual to be adopted; and

(8) the name of any person whose consent to the adoption is required, but who has not consented, and facts or circumstances which excuse the lack of his consent normally required to the adoption.

(b) A certified copy of the birth certificate or verification of birth record of the invididual to be adopted, if available, and the required consents and relinquishments shall be filed with the clerk.

Commissioners' Note

The language "including those available under a subsidy agreement" in subdivision (6) of subsection (a) was added in 1971 and is a recognition that an agreement between the adoptive parents and a social agency providing financial assistance to the adoptive parents in the event of adoption of the child is a recognizable resource of the adoptive parents. The use of subsidy agreements is a device which has come into prominence since the Revised Uniform Adoption Act was approved by the National Conference.

The language "or verification of

birth record" in subsection (6) was added in 1971 and permits verification of birth record, an inexpensive document commonly used as evidence of birth, to serve to identify the adopted child.

Amendments

Subsec. (a)(6) was amended in 1971 by adding the phrase "including those available under a subsidy agreement".

Subsec. (b) was amended in 1971 by adding the words "or verification of birth record".

§ 10. [Report of Petitioner's Expenditures]

(a) Except as specified in subsection (b), the petitioner in any proceeding for the adoption of a minor shall file, before the petition is heard, a full accounting report in a manner acceptable to the Court of all disbursements of anything of value made or agreed to be made by or on behalf of the petitioner in connection with the adoption. The report shall show any expenses incurred in connection with:

(1) the birth of the minor;

(2) placement of the minor with petitioner;

(3) medical or hospital care received by the mother or by the minor during the mother's prenatal care and confinement; and

(4) services relating to the adoption or to the placement of the minor for adoption which were received by or on behalf of the petitioner, either natural parent of the minor, or any other person.

(b) This section does not apply to an adoption by a step-parent whose spouse is a natural or adoptive parent of the child.

(c) Any report made under this section must be signed and verified by the petitioner.

Commissioners' Note

This section is taken from section 224(r) of the California Civil Code. The only adoption to which the section is inapplicable is an adoption by a step-parent.

The purpose of this section is to control some of the abuses which appear from time to time in "private placements" by requiring the petitioner to reveal expenditures which he has made in connection with the adoption. The section does not invalidate the adoption nor make it impossible for the petitioner to adopt the child because, as an example, in return for the prospective mother's promise to consent to adoption he agreed and paid medical expenses of the mother or any other payments to the mother.

§ 11. [Notice of Petition, Investigation and Hearing]

(a) After the filing of a petition to adopt a minor, the Court shall fix a time and place for hearing the petition. At least 20 days before the date of hearing, notice of the filing of the petition and of the time and place of hearing shall be given by the petitioner to (1) [Public Welfare Department]; (2) any agency or person whose consent to the adoption is required by this Act but who has not consented; and (3) a person whose consent is dispensed with upon any ground mentioned in paragraphs (1), (2), (6), (8), and (9) of subsection (a) of section 6 but who has not consented. The notice to [Public Welfare Department] shall be accompanied by a copy of the petition.

(b) An investigation shall be made by the [Public Welfare Department] or any other qualified agency or person designated by the Court to inquire into the conditions and antecedents of a minor sought to be adopted and of the petitioner for the purpose of ascertaining whether the adoptive home is a suitable home for the minor and whether the proposed adoption is in the best interest of the minor.

(c) A written report of the investigation shall be filed with the Court by the investigator before the petition is heard.

(d) The report of the investigation shall contain an evaluation of the placement with a recommendation as to the granting of the petition for adoption and any other information the Court requires regarding the petitioner or the minor.

(e) Unless directed by the Court, an investigation and report is not required in cases in which an agency is a party or joins in person to be adopted is an adult. In other cases, the Court may waive the investigation only if it appears that waiver is in the best interest of the minor and that the adoptive home and the minor are suited to each other. The ¿Public Welfare Department¡ which is required to consent to the adoption may give consent without making the investigation.

(f) The [Public Welfare Department] or the agency or persons designated by the Court to make the required investigation may request other departments or agencies within or without this state to make investigations of designated portions of the inquiry as may be appropriate and to make a written report thereof as a supplemental report to the Court and shall make similar investigations and reports on behalf of other agencies or persons designated by the Courts of this state or another place.

(g) After the filing of a petition to adopt an adult the Court by order shall direct that a copy of the petition and a notice of the time and place of the hearing be given to any person whose consent to the adoption is required but who has not consented. The court may order an appropriate investigation to assist it in determining whether the adoption is in the best interest of the persons involved.

(h) Notice shall be given in the manner appropriate under rules of civil procedure for the service of process in a civil action in this state or in any manner the Court by order directs. Proof of the giving of the notice shall be filed with the Court before the petition is heard.

Commissioners' Note

This section establishes the procedure for notices, investigations, and hearings.

Subsection (a) lists the persons who must be given notice of the petition. Normally in an agency placement, the consents will have bben obtained before filing of the petition so that no notice need be given. Subsection (a) (3) does require notice be given to a person whose consent is going to be dispensed with on any of the grounds listed in section 6(a) (1) and (2). There will be cases where the consents have not been obtained or where the petitioner chooses to obtain the consents in the presence of the court during the proceedings and this section makes provisions for obtaining the consents after filing of the petition.

Subsection (b) and following sections require, unless dispensed with by the court, or other circumstances, that an investigation be made by a designated person to determine whether the adoptive home is a suitable home for the minor and whether the proposed adoption is in the best interest of the minor. In an agency placement, the investigation may well have been done prior to the filing of the petition. In private placements, the first opportunity to secure knowledge of the existence of the child may arise as a result of the adoption petition.

Section 12 requires the minor to be resident in the adoptive home for at least 6 months. The commencement of the 6 month period is, under section 12, either the placement by the agency or, in the case of private placements, notification of the fact of custody of the child by the petitioner to the public welfare department.

Subsection (c) requires the report of the investigation to contain a recommendation as to the granting of the petition. The assumption of this section is that the court is entitled to the "expert" judgment of the placement agency or other official making the investigation as well as a report by him of the bare facts.

§ 12. [Required Residence of Minor]

A final decree of adoption shall not be issued and an interlocutory decree of adoption does not become final, until the minor to be adopted, other than a stepchild of the petitioner, has lived in the adoptive home for at least 6 months after placement by an agency, or for at least 6 months after the [Public Welfare Department] or the Court has been informed of the custody of the minor by the petitioner, and the department or Court has had an opportunity to observe or investigate the adoptive home.

91

As indicated in the comment to section 11, this section gives an advantage to agency placement over independent placements. For agency placements, the adoption decree may be entered not less than 6 months after placement by the agency. For independent placements, the commencement of the 6 months period is not the initial custody of the child, but is the time that the department or court has been informed of the custody of the child by the petitioner. Thus, for speedy adoptions an advantage is given either to agency placement or to early notice to the official agencies of the fact of an independent placement.

Many attempts have been made to treat with the so-called "black market" adoption where the adoptive parents enter a state where the child is and take the child to another state for the adoptive home and there is no supervision of the initial placement. Any penalty on adotion by this procedure, however, improper it may be, which prohibits the issuance of an adoption decre may, in fact, work against the best interest of the child if the adoptive home is suitable and desirable for the child. The "penalty" imposed by this section is simply a penalty arising from any failure to give early notice to the supervisory agency in the state where the adoptive home is located. Adoption cannot occur until 6 months after the notice has been given.

§ 13. [Appearance; Continuance; Disposition of Petition]

(a) The petitioner and the individual to be adopted shall appear at the hearing on the petition, unless the presence of either is excused by the Court for good cause shown.

(b) The Court may continue the hearing from time to time to permit further observation, investigation, or consideration of any facts or circumstances affecting the granting of the petition.

(c) If at the conclusion of the hearing the Court determines that the required consents have been obtained or excused and that the adoption is in the best interest of the individual to be adopted, it may (1) issue a final decree of adoption; or (2) issue an interlocutory decree of adoption which by its own terms automatically becomes a final decree of adoption on a day therein specified, which day shall not be less than 6 months nor more than one year from the date of issuance of the decree, unless sooner vacated by the Court for good cause shown.

(d) If the requirements for a decree under subsection (c) have not been met, the court shall dismiss the petition and determine the person to have custody of the minor, including the petitioners if in the best interest of the minor. In an interlocutory decree of adoption the Court may provide for observation, investigation, and further report on the adoptive home during the interlocutory period.

Commissioners' Note

This section permits both a final decree of adoption and the entry of an "interlocutory decree" of adoption which ripens automatically into a final decree unless vacated by the court for good cause shown. A number of states have found that the interlocutory decree procedure permits closer supervision of the adoptive home during the initial period and regularizes the relationship between adoptive parents and child prior to entry of the final decree. This section authorizes the use of that procedure. On the other hand, nothing in this section prevents a court from delaying the hearing for the purpose of investigation or supervision rather than issuing an interlocutory decree to be followed by investigation and supervision.

§ 14. [Effect of Petition and Decree of Adoption]

(a) A final decree of adoption and an interlocutory decree of adoption which has become final, whether issued by a Court of this state or of any other place, have the following effect as to matters within the jurisdiction or before a court of this state:

(1) except with respect to a spouse of the petitioner and relatives of the spouse, to relieve the natural parents of the adopted individual of all parental rights and responsibilities,

and to terminate all legal relationships between the adopted individual and his relatives, including his natural parents, so that the adopted individual thereafter is a stranger to his former relatives for all purposes including inheritance and the interpretation or construction of documents, statutes, and instruments, whether executed before or after the adoption is decreed, which do not expressly include the individual by name or by some designation not based on a parent and child or blood relationship; and

(2) to create the relationship of parent and child between petitioner and the adopted individual, as if the adopted individual were a legitimate blood descendant of the petitioner, for all purposes including inheritance and applicability of statutes, documents, and instruments, whether executed before or after the adoption is decreed, which do not expressly exclude an adopted individual from their operation or effect.

(b) Notwithstanding the provisions of subsection (a), if a parent of a child dies without the relationship of parent and child having been previously terminated and a spouse of the living parent therefore adopts the child, the child's right of inheritance from or through the deceased parent is unaffected by the adoption.

(c) An interlocutory decree of adoption, while it is in force, has the same legal effect as a final decree of adoption. If an interlocutory decree of adoption is vacated, it shall be as though void from its issuance, and the rights, liabilities, and status of all affected persons which have not become vested shall be governed accordingly.

Commissioners' Note

This section is designed to terminate all relationship of the child to his blood relatives after entry of the interlocutory decree of adoption and to establish at that moment for all purposes the relationship of parent and child between the adoptive parents and the child. The purpose of this section is to give a statutory definition of the "child," for purposes of all statutes, documents, instruments, and the like, which is to govern all situations in which an expressed provision to the contrary is not made. It is not intended by this section to make the property rights of an adopted child a matter of contract; rather the purpose of the section is to make the person a child for all purposes and leave it to other law, such as the law of inheritance, to determine what the property rights of a chid are. By providing a statutory definition for child, the section is intended to make any use of the word "child" or other similar designation such as "issue," in an instrument include an adopted child unles the instrument expressly provides to the contrary.

The termination of relationship of parent and child between the adopted person and his natural parents and the family of the natural parents follows the trend of modern statutes and is desirable for many reasons. It eases the transition from old family to new family by providing for a clean final "cutoff" of legal relationships with the old family. It also preserves the secrecy of adoption proceedings as provided in section 16 by reducing the selfish reaons an individual might have to discover his antecedents.

§ 15. [Appeal and Validation of Adoption Decree]

(a) An appeal from any final order or decree rendered under this Act may be taken in the manner and time provided for appeal from a [judgment in a civil action.]

(b) Subject to the disposition of an appeal, upon the expiration of one year after an adoption decree is issued the decree cannot be questioned by any person including the petitioner, in any manner upon any ground, including fraud, misrepresentation, failure to give any required notice, or lack of jurisdiction of the parties or of the subject matter, unless, in the case of the adoption of a minor the petition has not taken custody of the minor, or, in the case of the adoption of an adult, the adult had no knowledge of the decree within the [one] year period.

Commissioners' Note

Subsection (b) is designed to impose a very short statute of limitation on an ability to upset a decree of adoption for any

95

failure to comply with the requirements of this Act, including failure of jurisdiction, fraud, or failure to give notice. The policy of stability in a family relationship, particularly when a young minor is involved, outweighs the possible loss to a person whose rights are cut off through fraud and ignorance.

§ 16. [Hearings and Records in Adoption Proceedings; Confidential Nature]

Notwithstanding any other law concerning public hearing and records,

(1) all hearings held in proceedings under this Act shall be held in closed Court without admittance of any person other than essential officers of the court, the parties, their witnesses, counsel, persons who have not previously consented to the adoption but are required to consent, and representatives of the agencies present to perform their offical duties; and

(2) all papers and records pertaining to the adoption whether part of the permanent record of the court or of a file in the [Department of Welfare] or in an agency are subject to inspection only upon consent of the Court and all interested persons; or in exceptional cases, only upon an order of the Court for good cause shown; and

(3) except as authorized in writing by the adoptive parent, the adopted child, if [14] or more years of age, or upon order of the court for good cause shown in exceptional cases, no person is required to disclose the name or identity of either an adoptive parent or an adopted child.

Commissioners' Note

The opening phrase is designed to negate the impact of any "right to know" law or other statute making public records open to inspection as a matter of right by newspapers and other persons. It continues the policy of existing adoption acts of making the proceedings confidential in nature.

Subdivision (3) was added in 1971 so that persons having knowledge of a particular adoption cannot be required without written authorization to disclose the name and identity of an adoptive parent or adopted child. This provision is intended to meet the problem presented in Anonymous v. Anonymous, 298 N.Y.S. 2d 345 (N.Y. 1969).

Amendments

Subsec. (3) added in 1971.

Action in Adopting Jurisdictions

Variations from Offical Text:

North Dakota. In subsec. (3), omits, "if [14] or more years of age".

§ 17. [Recognition of Foreign Decree Affecting Adoption]

A decree of court terminating the relationship of aprent and child or establishing the relationship by adoption issued pursuant to due process of law by a court of any other jurisdiction within or without the United States shall be recognized in this state and the rights and obligations of the parties as to matters within the jurisdiction of this state shall be determined as though the decree were issued by a court of this state.

Commissioners' Note

The purpose of this section is to require the courts of this state to recognize termination decrees and adoption decrees issued by courts of other places. It is designed to eliminate from litigation in this state any claim that the adoption was granted on grounds or jurisdiction not recognized in this state. Thus, if a foreign nation gives jurisdiction to grant an adoption on the basis of nationality of the petitioners or of the person to be adopted without regard to residence, the courts of this state are, nevertheless, instructed to recognize the

97

adoption decree. The decree should be given effect as if it were issued by the courts of this state. If in the state of issuance of an adoption decree the adopted child continues to have rights of inheritance from the natural parents, his rights, are, to the extent the law of this state is controlling, nevertheless cut off.

§ 18. [Application for New Birth Record]

Within 30 days after an adotion decree becomes final, the clerk of the court shall prepare an application for a birth record in the new name of the adopted individual and forward the application to the appropriate vital statistics office of the place, if known, where the adopted individual was born and forward a copy of the decree to the [Department of Welfare] of this state for statistical purposes.

Commissioners' Note

The clerk of the adoption court who has the official record of the adoption decree is directed by this section to secure the issuance of a new birth certificate. Nothing in this section prevents the agency participating in the adoption process from preparing the new certificate and forwarding it to the appropriate authorities via the clerk of the court.

§ 19. [Relinquishment and Termination of Parent and Child Relationship]

(a) The rights of a parent with reference to a child, including parental right to control the child or to withhold consent to an adoption, amy be relinquished and the relationship of parent and child terminated in or prior to an adoption proceeding as provided in this section.

(b) All rights of a parent with reference to a child, including the right to receive notice of a hearing on a petition for adoption, may be relinquished and the relationship of parent and child terminated by a writing, signed by the parent, regardless of the age of the parent,

(1) in the presence of a representative of an agency taking custody of the child, whether the agency is within or without

the state or in the presence and with the approval of a judge of a court of record within or without this state in which the minor was present or in which the parent resided at the time it was signed, which relinquishment may be withdrawn within 10 days after it is signed or the child is born, whichever is later; and the relinquishment is invalid unless it states that the parent has this right of withdrawal; or

(2) in any other situation if the petitioner has had custody of the minor for [2] years, but only if notice of the adoption proceeding has been given to the parent and the court finds, after considering the circumstances of the relinquishment and the long continued custody by the petitioner, that the best interest of the child requires the granting of the adoption.

(c) In addition to any other proceeding provided by law, the relationship of parent and child may be terminated by a court order issued in connection with an adoption proceeding under this Act on any ground provided by other law for termination of the relationship, and in any event on the ground (1) that the minor has been abandoned by the parent, (2) that the reason of the misconduct, faults, or habits of the parent or the repeated and continuous neglect or refusal of the parent, the minor is without proper parental care and control, or subsistence, education or other care or control necessary for his physical, mental, or emotional health or morals, or by, reason of physical or mental incapacity the parent is unable to provide necessary parental care for the minor, and the court finds that the conditions and causes of the behavior, neglect, or incapacity are irremediable or will not be remedied by the parent, and tht by reason thereof the minor is suffering or probably will suffer serious physical, mental, moral, or emotional harm, or (3) that in the case of a parent not having custody of a minor, his consent is being un-reasonably withheld contrary to the best interest of the minor.

(d) For the purpose of proceeding under this Act, a decree terminating all rights of a parent with reference to a child or the relationship of parent and child issued by a court of competent jurisdiction in this or any other state dispenses with the consent to adoption proceedings of a parent whose rights or parent and child relationship are terminated by the decree and with any required notice of an adoption proceeding other than as provided in this section.

(e) A petition for termination of the relationships of parent and child made in connection with an adoption proceeding may be made by:

(1) either parent if termination of the relationship is sought with respect to the other parent;

(2) the petitioner for adoption, the guardian of the person, the legal custodian of the child, or the individual standing in parental relationship to the child;

(3) an agency; or

(4) any other person having a legitimate interest in the matter.

(f) Before the petition is heard, notice of the hearing thereon and opportunity to be heard shall be given the parents of the child, the guardian of the person of the child, the person having legal custody of the child, and, in the discretion of the court, a person appointed to represent any party.

(g) Notwithstanding the provisions of subsection (b), a relinquishment of parental rights with respect to a child, executed under this section, may be withdrawn by the parent, and a decree of a court terminating the parent and child relationship under this section may be vacated by the Court upon motion of the parent, if the child is not on placement for adoption and the person having custody of the child consents in writing to the withdrawal or vacation of the decree.

Commissioners' Note

This section supplies an important omission from a number of earlier adoption acts. Many acts make no provision for relinquishing or terminating the requirement of consent by a parent. While a number of states provided in the Juvenile Court Act or elsewhere in the statutory law a procedure for termination of parental rights, there was noting in the Adoption Act requiring recognition of such proceedings as a method of eliminating the requirement of parental consent.

This section provides two methods of eliminating the necessity of consent by a parent: voluntary relinquishment of parental rights under subsection (b) by a writing signed by the parent; and a court order terminating parental rights under subsection (c) on the grounds specified in that section. Subsection (c) lists the persons who may petition for termination of parental rights in connection with an adoption proceeding. Nothing in this listing of persons who may be petitioners limits the provisions in the Juvenile Court or other acts specifying other or additional persons who may petition for termination of parental rights under those acts where no adoption proceeding is pending.

The grounds for terminating parental rights in subsection (c) are more inclusive than the grounds proposed in the Children's Bureau pamphlet referred to in the comment to section 1 and are taken from statutes such as those in California and Wisconsin. The final ground listed in subsection (c) concerns unreasonable withholding of consent to adoption. It can be used in a case where a step-parent and the mother are in custody of the child but the natural father refuses to give consent and withholding of consent is found by the court to be contrary to the best interests of the child. It cannot be used, however, to excuse the absence of consent of a parent who is in legal control of his child or who has custody of the child.

§ 20. [Uniformity of Interpretation]

This Act shall be so interpreted and construed as to effectuate its general purpose to make uniform the law of those states which enact it.

§ 21. [Short Title]

This Act may be cited as the Revised Uniform Adoption Act.

Library References

Adoption ⬤⟲ 3.   C.J.S. Adoption of Persons §§ 6, 7.

§ 22. [Repeal and Effective Date]

(a) The following acts and laws are repealed as of the effective date of this Act:

(1)

(2)

(3)

(b) Any adoption or termination proceedings pending on the effective date of this Act is not affected thereby.

§ 23. [Time of Taking Effect]

This Act shall take effect . . . .

APPENDIX C

Standards of Practice for Adoption Services

New York State
Department of Social Services

Section 455.1 Principles of adoption services.

(a) Each child deprived of a permanent family shall be provided with an adoptive family in which he may have the opportunity for growth and development through loving care, parental guidance, and the security of a permanent home.

(b) Efforts to remove a child from the care and custody of his biological parent, adoptive parent, or legal guardian shall be undertaken only when it is clearly established that such action is in his best interest.

(c) The rights of children, biological parents, legal guardians, foster parents and adoptive families shall be respected and protected through compliance with appropriate laws, rules and regulations and through responsible agency administration.

(d) Each child under care in need of adoption but not legally free for placement shall be identified as early as possible and the legal process to sever those parental or guardianship rights of custody and guardianship to the child impeding his or her speedy placement in an adoptive family shall be initiated.

Section 455.2 Definitions. For the purpose of this part, the following definitions shall apply.

(a) "Adoption services" mean a service for a child who is in need of adoption.

(b) "Biological parent" means an expectant parent, or a parent (married or unmarried, adult or minor) of a child conceived or born in or out of wedlock.

(c) "Child" means a person actually or apparently under the age of 18 years either surrendered by his biological parent, adoptive parent or guardian or free for adoption as a result of a

103

judicial finding of permanent neglect or of abandonment, or not surrendered but placed in the care of the agency, or not surrendered and remaining with the biological parent or adoptive parent receiving ongoing service, or for whom guardianship has otherwise been granted pursuant to section 384 of the Social Services Law.

(d)　"Adoptive applicant" means a single person or married person who has applied to adopt or who has received agency approval for the placement of a child in his, her, or their home for the purpose of adoption.

(e)　"Adoptive parent" means a single person or married person with whom a child has been placed for adoption or who has adopted a child with agency approval.

(f)　"Legal guardian" means a person to whom or an agency to which the guardianship of the person of a child has been committed by surrender or in accordance with the terms of a surrender instrument or pursuant to a court order under Section 384 of the Social Services Law. A legal guardian may also be a person appointed as guardian of the person of a child pursuant to a duly executed will or deed as provided by Section 81 of the Domestic Relations Law.

(g)　"Foster parent" means a single person or married person with whom a child has been placed on a boarding home basis in a certified or licensed foster home.

(h)　"Authorized agency" means any agency, association, corporation, institution, society or other organization which is incorporated or organized under the laws of this State with corporate power or empowered by law to care for, to place out or to board out children, which actually has its place of business or plant in this State and which is approved, visited, inspected and supervised by the State Board of Social Welfare or which shall submit and consent to the approval, visitation, inspection and supervision of the Board as to any and all acts in relation to the welfare of children performed or to be performed under the Social Services Law. An authorized agency shall also mean any court or any social services official of this State authorized by law to place out or to board out children.

Section 455.3 General requirements.

(a) Authorized agencies providing adoption service shall:

    1. have written policies and procedures governing service to:
       (i) biological parents, legal guardians, adoptive parents and adoptive applicants;

       (ii) children who are free for adoption, or who are not free but in need of adoptive planning.

    2. have written policies pertaining to:
       (i) agency recruitment, approval, and supervision of adoptive homes until adoption proceedings are completed;

       (ii) services after adoption proceedings are completed.

    3. make provisions for those written policies to be available to any interested party and to be provided to biological parents, adoptive applicants, legal guardians and foster parents.

    4. make explicit the criteria by which the agency decides upon the suitability of a prospective adoptive home, including such matters as the agency's policy regarding placement, e.g., transracial placement, single parent adoptions, placements in homes where the mother works, and that in evaluating the suitability of a potential home the agency will consider such factors as the stability of the marriage and the ability of the applicants to care for a child not born to them.

    5. within the limitation imposed by Section 373 of the Social Services Law and Section 116 of the Family Court Act, provide for flexible methods for evaluation and selection of adoptive applicants and periodic review of eligibility requirements; however, in no instance shall an agency's decision be arbitrary in the use of such factors as age, race, religious tenets, religious affiliations or lack thereof, previous divorce, income, sterility, infertility or a non-disabling health problem.

    6. maintain appropriate records demonstrating compliance with approved policies and procedures; maintain a written

narrative record for each child and adoptive applicant containing information which shall be used to substantiate decisions and plans of action.

7. provide appropriate orientation, in-service training and supervision for agency staff assigned to adoption service, and make available a copy of the *New York State Department of Social Services Adoption Guide* to each worker at the time of assignment.

8. develop and maintain positive relationships with interested persons, citizens' groups, agencies, persons in related disciplines and professional groups who have responsibility for certain functions or render services related to adoption.

9. have a public information program which shall:
    (i) inform the community about the children under care in need of adoption;
    (ii) inform the community about the agency's adoption policies and service;
    (iii) endeavor to promote community understanding, knowledge, and support of the program for adoptions with subsidy and/or medical subsidy; and
    (iv) offer orientation about the agency program to organizations, agencies, media representatives, and other persons who represent referral sources in the community.

(b) The policies of each Social Services District shall be reviewed annually by the local Social Services Commissioner and a written record kept that such review has been made even when there is no change in policy.

(c) The policies of each voluntary agency shall be reviewed annually by its Board of Directors with its Executive Directors and a written record kept that such review has been made even when there is no change in policy.

Section 455.4 Agency Requirements.

(a) In providing adoption services to biological parents and legal guardians, authorized agencies shall:

106

1. endeavor to provide immediate services to any biological parent or legal guardian coming to the agency on his, her or their own initiative or referred by a person or agency in the community. These services shall include discussion of alternatives to adoption in making the best plan for the child and parent. The medical, social and casework services provided may include such items as day care, counseling, job training and housing. There may be referral to other agencies when indicated.

2. offer services with the recognition of each person's inherent dignity, integrity and right to privacy, and with the assurance that discussion and exploration of personal problems shall be kept confidential and confined to one agency worker as far as possible.

3. assure the referent of the biological parent or legal guardian of the readiness to give prompt service. If appropriate, the agency shall inform the referent whether the biological parent or legal guardian kept the appointment.

4. respect the right and responsibility of the biological parent or legal guardian to establish a plan for the child. The biological parent and the legal guardian shall be advised of the guardianship and custody provisions of Section 384 of the Social Services Law, of the provisions of periodic family court review under Section 392 of the Social Services Law and of the provisions for permanent neglect proceedings under Section 611 of the Family Court Act.

5. give definite regular appointments at reasonably frequent intervals. If an appointment is not kept, the caseworker shall endeavor to contact the biological parent or legal guardian immediately, making a home visit when appropriate and recording as a permanent part of the record the reason why the appointment was not kept, when known.

6. after referring a biological parent or legal guardian to another community resource for service, ascertain the outcome of the referral as soon as practicable. When a report from a medical or psychiatric resource indicates the biological parent or legal guardian failed to keep the appointment or failed to contact the community resource, the

agency shall make a diligent effort to reach the biological parent or legal guardian to determine the current situation, the reason for failing to contact the resource, and the need for further agency service.

7. with regard to the role of the biological father, recognize the rights and interest of the father in planning for the child.

8. comply with the following surrender procedures:

   (i) a surrender shall be effected when requested by the biological parent or legal guardian and shall not be dependent upon the child's adoptability or any factor other than the readiness of the biological parent or legal guardian to surrender the child. However, the agency shall impress upon the biological parent or legal guardian the child's paramount need for speed in establishing permanent family relationships;

   (ii) before accepting a surrender be satisfied that the biological parent or legal guardian has a full understanding of the plan and of the religious faith requirements of Section 373 of the Social Services Law;

   (iii) there shall be a separate signed statement of the religious wishes of the surrendering person as to the placement of the child. This statement shall advise the parent or guardian of the right to express the wish that the child be placed in a family of the same religion as the parent or of a different religion from the parent or with indifference to religion or with religion a subordinate consideration. In addition, the statement shall make explicit to the surrendering person that if he or she wishes to do so, he or she may express the wish that if no home has been found for the child within the number of months to be specified by that person, then the placement of the child shall be made without reference to those expressed religious wishes which may be impeding placement;

   (iv) the terms of a surrender and its execution shall meet the requirements of Section 384 of the Social Services Law;

(v) where an agency has occasion to believe that because of a language problem, the person surrendering the child may not fully understand the surrender instrument or the provision therein relating to prohibition against proceeding for recovery of the child when 30 days have elapsed after the execution of the surrender or the right to express a religious preference as specified in Section 35.4(a) (8) (iii) then the agency shall obtain a separate signed statement (to be included as part of the permanent records of the agency) in a language understood by that person which shall establish that the agency has fully explained these matters to the surrendering person.

(b) In providing adoption services for children, authorized agencies shall:

1. recognize that any child who is legally free is adoptable.

2. obtain thorough knowledge and understanding of the development, health, medical history, family life, family history and social experience for each child admitted to agency care; and for each child accepted for adoption services obtain sufficient information to make a determination as to the best setting for his growth and development; obtain all authorizations for care and for release of medical and social information concerning the child and the parent(s).

3. arrange a medical examination for each child for whom adoption is planned in order to determine the state of the child's health, significant factors that may interfere with normal development, and the implications of any medical problems; the medical report shall be filed in the child's record.

4. make every diligent effort to find a permanent home for a child who has been surrendered by his biological parent or legal guardian or has been legally freed through court process.

5. register each child with the State Adoption Exchange in accordance with the Regulations of the State Department of Social Services.

6. provide casework service for each child accepted and maintain current understanding of his or her needs and encourage his or her participation in planning according to his or her age and capacity.

7. utilize all available professional and paraprofessional skills as may be appropriate.

8. consider the availability of an adoption subsidy under Section 398.6(k) of the Social Services Law where appropriate.

9. keep the length of interim foster care placements of children free for adoption to a minimum, placing such children in adoptive homes as early as practicable.

(c) In providing services to adoptive parents authorized agencies shall:

1. Maintain a record of initial inquiries from potential adoptive applicants and formal applications showing date, name, address and disposition.

2. use of formal adoption application requiring signatures from the applicant.

3. inform adoptive applicants of the home study process.

4. (i) make an early disposition on each application, advising applicants in writing of the receipt of the application within five working days after it is submitted;

(ii) discuss at the initial meeting with adoptive applicant the children available for adoption, emphasizing children with special needs, handicapped and minority race children and the resources available for locating such children, including the State Adoption Exchange, and that applicants interested in such children may be given priority;

(iii) inform the applicants accepted for home study of the approximate time when the study shall begin and the reasons for any delay;

(iv) advise applicants who have not been accepted for home study of the reasons for such action.

5. arrange for an adoptive study of each accepted adoptive applicant as early as possible.

6. arrange interviews with adoptive applicant, individually and jointly, including at least one visit to the applicant's home.

7. complete a homestudy once initiated within a period not to exceed four months unless there are delays by mutual consent or due to circumstances beyond the control of the agency, in which case such circumstances shall be stated in writing to the applicant.

8. remind each applicant approved for adoptive placement of the purpose and registration requirements of the State Adoptive Exchange when the agency has no children available for placement for the approved applicant.

9. establish a homestudy process to insure that agency decisions regarding homestudy approvals or disapprovals shall not rest with one individual.

10. if an agency decision has been made either to discontinue a homestudy or disapprove an applicant for adoptive placement, offer a personal interview with the adoptive applicant(s) and the reasons for discontinuance or disapproval shall be part of the permanent written records of the agency.

11. recognize the needs of the child to be adopted as the primary criteria in determining the selection of an adoptive family for the child and that the family's capacity to nurture that child shall be among the major considerations in the choice of an adoptive home.

(d) Each authorized agency shall make the following special provisions for adoption services:

1. provide for the right of foster parent to a preference under Social Services Law 383.3; and incorporate in all written foster parent placement agreements a statement of the

111

preference of foster parents as required under Section 374.1-a of the Social Services Law.

2. notify the foster parents caring for such child whenever it initiates a proceeding to obtain the guardianship and custody of a child pursuant to Section 384 of the Social Services Law.

3. maintain a program for selection, review and acceptance of applications for study which shall provide for:

   (i) ongoing systematic review of the children under care of the agency and those children listed on the State Adoption Exchange to determine kinds of homes needed;

   (ii) the consideration of the needs of available children in determining which adoptive applicants shall be accepted for study;

   (iii) preference to be given to families willing to take immediately available children.

4. Special provisions for adoptive placement. Each authorized agency shall:

   (i) prior to the initial visit, insure that the potential adoptive parents(s) have opportunity to discuss and be fully informed about the child;

   (ii) arrange the initial visit of the child with the prospective adoptive parent(s) at a time and place appropriate for all;

APPENDIX D

Procedures for Foreign Adoptions

Each international adoption is somewhat different, even adoptions arranged by the same agency, but there are some usual steps that almost everyone attempting to adopt from abroad will take. They are outlined here in broad form. You will of course have to get specific information from whatever contact you use about particular programs.

First, however we should mention the general types of international contacts for adoption:

1. Adoption through an established licensed agency in the United States.

2. Adoption through an agency abroad, perhaps with the aid of a formal or informal U.S. contact or support group.

3. An independent adoption arranged directly by the adoptive parents and/or their lawyer with a foreign contact such as an orphanage director, doctor, lawyer, personal friend, or others. These do not usually ask for a homestudy.

In all three types, the aim is to locate, legally obtain custody of, adopt, and bring into the United States on a permanent basis a child, usually orphaned or abandoned, who is not a U.S. citizen.

Steps to take:

1. Check with your state department of welfare or other state agency governing adoptions: What are the adoption regulations of your state? What are the policies governing foreign adoptions? Are there specific agencies to contact or policies to follow? If you do not meet these requirements, you may not be able to obtain a preferential visa for your child (which saves a long wait on a quota list) unless you physically see the child before applying for a visa. For a couple, this means that both of you will have to travel to see the child.

2. Starting with local agencies first, find out which licensed adoption agencies in your state will do homestudies for foreign adoptions. In some areas, public agencies will do these; in other areas, only private agencies will. Agencies also vary as to what types of foreign placements they will handle and which international agencies they will work with. If you plan to move across state lines, check with your new state about regulations and whether your homestudy will be transferrable.

3. At the same time, contact groups working with foreign adoptions. Some private (independent) contacts may not ask for

113

homestudies, but your state still may. Agencies abroad may ask after they assign a child to you rather than before. Sometimes local adoption agencies will not do a homestudy for you until you are accepted as a prospective adoptive parent by an international program. But some international programs will not accept you until you can show a completed study. This type of situation can be circumvented by having one write a letter to the other saying that you would be considered for adoption pending their action.

4. Narrow down to three or four programs that interest you and write to them for information. Based on their replies, choose two that fit your needs, and that you also fit as an applicant, and apply. But notify them that you wish to apply to other programs. If neither works out, try your next choices.

5. After one of the programs accepts your application, asks for and receives your homestudy; or after your homestudy is sent to the program with your application and you are approved; or after you have sent preliminary papers to a foreign contact or agency and been approved—you will *wait*. How long you wait depends upon the program, the available children, and your requests and background.

6. Finally, information on a child, and usually a picture, is sent to you either directly or through your agency or lawyer. If for good reason you decide that you cannot accept this child, you will possibly be assigned another child at a later date. If you accept a child, documents will be exchanged so that you can begin the adoption and immigration proceedings. With many foreign contacts, you will be required to travel to pick up the child and may have to spend time in the child's country to arrange legal matters. U.S. agencies do not usually require this.

7. Contact the nearest U.S. Immigration and Naturalization Office to determine the type of visa your child will need for entry into the United States. Most couples will obtain an I-600 form, "Petition to Classify Orphan as Immediate Relative." It asks for a preferential visa on the basis that an orphaned or half-orphaned child under the age of fourteen will be adopted by a couple at least one of whom is a citizen. A couple will fill it out and submit it with: child's birth certificate, parents' birth certificates, proof of orphanage, fingerprints of parents, marriage certificate, and financial statements. An I-600 takes four to eight weeks to process normally, and a health check must be done by a U.S. Public Health Service official on the child abroad. Families who will travel abroad and see the child do not have to prove they meet state requirements for adoption and may shorten processing time.

8. You will not be able to use an I-600 visa if: you are single; you

have already used two I-600 visas; neither spouse is a citizen; the child has two living parents; the child is over fourteen. Unless you are willing to wait out the quota, you must find some other type of preferential visa such as medical students, visitors, or special act of Congress introduced by your congressman.

9. When the papers have been approved by immigration officials, they are sent or you bring them to the U.S. consul nearest your child overseas. The consul then has the power to issue the visa.

10. Once the visa has been issued and an exit visa issued to the child by the foreign country of which he is a citizen, *and* if all the adoption proceedings or other necessary matters as outlined by the program or contact are completed, your child is ready to go home.

11. How long it takes to prepare for the journey depends upon the health of the child, how efficient the program is, and the availability of escorts and flights. If you escort your own child, you should make sure you both have passports and identification in order.

12. After arrival in the United States, you must register your child as an alien every January with the INS since he or she is not a citizen.

13. After a minimum of six months you can file for legal adoption of your child in your state of residence. The adoption proceedings may differ slightly from domestic adoptions, so check with your courts.

14. Two years after legal adoptions, your child is eligible for naturalization as a U.S. citizen.

INDEX

LEGAL ALMANAC SERIES CONVERSION TABLE
List of Original Titles and Authors

LEGAL ALMANAC SERIES CONVERSION TABLE
List of Present Titles and Authors